The Way of Ducks

a cottage devotional

Laurie Lamb

THE WAY OF DUCKS

ISBN-10: 1-926676-17-3
ISBN-13: 978-1-926676-17-3

Printed by Word Alive Press

131 Cordite Road, Winnipeg, MB R3W 1S1
www.wordalivepress.ca

Printed in Canada.

Dedication

One day in early June, in my own sad loneliness and self-imposed isolation, a family of ducks came into my life. “Momma” and eight soft fuzzy babies drifted onto our shore. As I learned to feed them and reach out to touch them, something was reaching into me, soothing my anxiety and touching my heart.

I spent that summer sitting on the dock, watching momma raise her young and learning to understand the nuances of their behavior. Many times I realized I had spent a whole afternoon, which before may have felt lonely, in the delightful company of "momma" and her growing family. I remember one Saturday morning I was feeling so lost and separated from my own family when suddenly I realized that God had given me this little family of ducks to heal and restore me. God is the one who loves us enough to know us and our inmost being. He cares for us so deeply and is the only one who can touch our brokenness and transform our pain into joy.

Over that summer I developed a bond with these ducks. I grew to recognize each one of them by their markings and behavior. Momma was by far the most endearing and dedicated parent. Her commitment to her young and her fierce protection of them amazed me. I would appear on the dock and call and she would answer, sometimes coming from as far as the beach. Many times she waddled up the walkway loudly looking for a hand-out. There were others in the extended group, Bossy and Dinty, orphaned young and other older males.

The summer was flying by and like last year, momma would soon be leaving. One afternoon late in August, as I sat in the sun with my feet dangling in the water watching them gobble seed off the sandy bottom, I heard a voice as clear as though someone was sitting beside me, "What have you done with what I gave you?" I felt compelled to write about all these interactions with the ducks and so the writing began as fall approached and the time with momma was growing short.

I dedicate this "little" book to my brother Richard, who when he was dying, tried to reach out and make amends. I saw someone who in sadness did not want to leave love behind. Dying people talk about love and kindness and sigh over all that they may have missed and are going to miss. We had no words to help us say those things that needed to be said but God creates beautiful bridges and I know one day I will get a great big hug from my brother - in glorious newness of life. (Titus 3: 4-5)

June 5th Year Two, It All Begins Again

Momma originally flew across the bay in early June. I recognized her dark streak through her eye to the side of her head. Her babies were safely under the willow branches by the beach. She flew right up on the lawn as if to make sure it was us. Last year and so many hundreds of miles over the winter and she was here – again. How I marveled at her tenacity, her fit in the cycle of nature. Where had she been, what marshy vistas and sweeping storms had she been in? Last year all her babies not only ate out of my hand but I could lift them from the water, feel delightful feet as they jumped back in the lake, from tiny golden fluff to adult duck. Did I dream it? Did they really share themselves with me? They were a healing to my soul, the bond so tenuous, the trust never broken.

It came to me afresh, listening to the song of the plain sparrow, hearing the lapping water, smelling the heat on the stone walkway, all is good in the world. Nature restores us; gives us perspective, shows us God's wisdom.

Who else has held the oceans in his hand? Who has measured off the heavens with his fingers?.... To whom then can we compare God?...22 he is the one who spreads out the heavens like a curtain and makes his tent from them.
Isaiah 40: 12

June 8th

I Remember Holding

How well I remember holding my hand out with seed, being so patient, waiting and waiting for the first hesitant baby to come close. As the water lapped at my hand, seed would float off and the babies would gobble it up. I realized that God was doing the same thing. He was so patiently holding out his hand, waiting and watching for me to take what he was offering. It was as if he was asking - "Will you trust me? Will you take what I am offering you? Will you come close and let me feed your soul?"

As day after day I watched for the ducks, my joy in life slowly began to come back. The soft, gentle morning air - the breath of God. The warm uneven stone of our sidewalk underfoot, the smell of fresh green growth and the murmur of baby ducks renewed in me a hope and an anticipation of each new day.

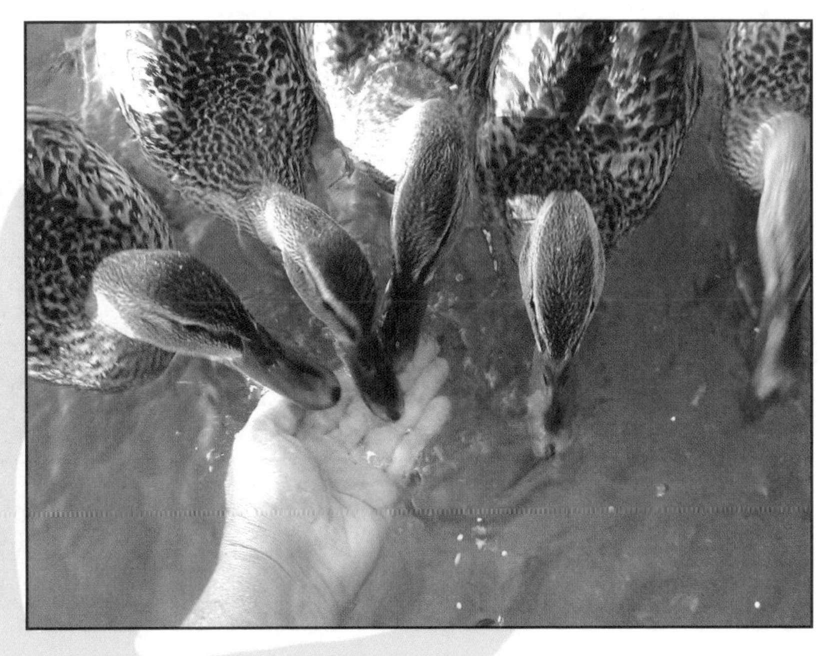

God gives us so much. Everything we touch has it's roots in Him. All goodness is His. Titus 2:11 - For the grace of God has been revealed, bringing salvation to all people.

June 10th
Small Voice

Once little momma lost her voice. She would hiss at me with her baby by her side. I was never sure if she was asking for food or if she was threatening me. One day her beak opened - no sound. Had I caused it - did seed get lodged in her throat? How would she call her baby, warn it or direct it? She was silent for a couple of days. I was so delighted to hear her "quack."

September 10th

Floating Seed

Sometimes I had to feed the ducks on either side of the dock. They would spend so much time chasing the others away, they would miss the floating seed and have to dive for it. How many times do we do that? -Keep others away and in the process miss out ourselves? We are called to a higher standard - love our brothers, help those who are less fortunate. How does God separate us?

October 2nd

God in the Darkness

This morning after weeks of rain and waves, while it was still mostly dark, I went down to the dock. The sun was only a vague light spot in the low clouds. How sweetly still and holy it felt. I threw seed over the area the ducks would later come to. The seed has a certain weight and it falls with a little splash. As I looked over the lake I saw momma and her new mate coming. What a surprise.

I think sometimes God is like that – coming to us out of the darkness – providing for us even before we know we're looking for it.

October 8th

Mink

These are the fall days now. It is not light until after 7 and the sidewalk is cold. Yesterday was a beautiful Indian Summer day – the bees and the odd dragonfly were buzzing. We had fed momma and her new boyfriend and were lazily soaking up the sun. I watched the mink run over the rocks – so brown and shiny. He disappeared under our jetty. Something clicked in my mind and I jumped up – the ducks were still feeding in the shallow water! I started yelling and clapping my hands. I saw the mink – such a strong, smooth, silent swimmer – skimming along the sandy bottom. Then an explosion of feathers and wings and squawks!

The mink snatched at the new male and missed. I was banging the dock and yelling. He hid under the jetty. Downy feathers were floating all over as the ducks set up their alarm – quacking in unison, intently watching the shore. A close call. All I could do was watch it happen and offer a warning.

How often does our Lord watch our interactions and near misses with danger? How often do we hear His voice calling a warning caution? How many times did you miss His call?

October 26th

Frost

Frost was on the ground. It shone white and crystal-like as the sun rose. I saw a fat male duck with the characteristic "ringtail" feathers so I went down to the dock. I thought I wasn't expecting him to swim over but I was disappointed when he swam a distance away and looked back. These are the tough ones – the ones who are staying the winter in the pond down the street, the ones who will rely on being fed by a kind man, safe in his winter pond. And yet, they have no trust.

Are they like the ones who profess they believe but somehow never experience the living, breathing God? What they are missing! How delighted I would have been to feed them, marveling at their buoyancy, their stretching wings and strong swimming feet. How God waits to be delighted in us. Have you missed a moment to bask in the breath of your loving Father?

November 30th

Early Light

I see the ducks swim by in the early light. The water is languid today, warm for the end of November. How soft and gentle the lake appears. I know if I go down to feed them, they will fly away. It is both foolish and safe. How do they know I am not a threat? My ducks know my voice, my size, my gestures. They know I am safe.

I am learning God's voice, his powerful and mighty presence, his gestures of wisdom, teaching – and sometimes – silence. Those are the times I'm tempted to fill with my own voice. Lord, help me not to fly away when you appear unfamiliar or too close for comfort. Help me trust you and build on what you've shown me. I know you only want to feed me and feel close to me.

I later realized how God is longing for us to return to him – like an ache to the heart.

December 5th

Ice Crystals

Snow and ice crystals cling to the rocks – at once beautiful and cold. The sun's soft pink rays warm to yellow on the snow. Steam will later rise off the rocks as water laps at their edges. Night will come and it will freeze again, as it has for eons past, since time began.

Are we like the rocks, warming to God's touch but cooling when darkness comes? How each new dawn should satisfy us. God is so reliable and trustworthy. Are you letting the waves of life confuse the certainty of God? Will you let him renew you each new day, warm you with His light?

December 8th

Last Geece

I watched a formation of geese rise out of the heavy white fog. They spread out through the air until they were evenly spaced. What co-operation! These are nearly the last ones. It is -17degrees today. The water will get that thick, glassy look soon, before it freezes. Snow flakes are large and fluffy and float down on a diagonal - so gently covering the ground and disappearing into the water. The geese standing on newly-exposed rocks will have snow-covered backs.

How poetic our God is. Sometimes we don't see our own poetic beauty but the One who observes everything does. When you feel flawed, inadequate or alone in this world where only beautiful people are noticed, remember the God who chose you sees you in all wisdom and love - for you.

December 11th

Cold and Ice

Many times the ducks are just swimming along the shore – either alone or as a pair. They're just doing what ducks do – paddling along looking for algae. They aren't seeking anything. If only they were looking or calling out, I would not mind the cold or the ice underfoot. How delighted I would be to greet them. I trudge down in my boots. To my surprise a pair is in the rock lagoon and turn to watch me. I throw the seed as far as I can. They want what I'm offering but are reluctant to put themselves at risk for it. I had to retreat up the walkway before they would come into the shallows for the seed. How many times would I have to do that before they would trust me and come looking?

How often are we all just drifting along – missing the hand of God extended?

December 19th

Time of Waiting

I walked down to the water. It was still and dark - a time of waiting. Lone snowflakes drifted down in the stillness. I turned and looked back at the house. The lights on our Christmas tree glowed so warmly through the window.

God's presence - as sure and quiet and warm. Times of waiting - knowing His plans are perfect.

December 20th

Venture Into Relationship

Some days I can't throw the seed out far enough for the ducks to venture into the shallow water. All it takes is one duck, usually a female with a mate, and the rest will follow.

God's display in nature is like the seed cast on the water. He hopes we will notice what He has created for us to enjoy and venture into relationship with him. It's as certain as seed floating with the breeze and as elusive when we can't overcome our hesitation.

The ducks have been so hungrily gobbling the seed, they forgot I was standing there watching them. There will come a time when we will need to approach him on his terms but through His grace he gives us freedom to come on our terms, when we are ready. How gently He throws his arms open to us. Can you venture into them?

December 21st

Seasons

Ice is on the rocks, crisp frost on the grass. The sunrise is clear and bright, glinting off the rhythm of waves. As beautiful as it is I am happy to get back inside to comfort and warmth. The sun shines on everything it touches. Some things reflect the light, others absorb it's warmth. The sunlight on the water reflects the movement of light over the ceiling. No wonder all things turn to the light.

Where would we be without the Light of the world? Every season has it's own rhythm -whether heat or cold, sun or cloud. How do we embrace the seasons in our lives? How easy is the warmth and freedom of summer, how much more protection we need in the cold of winter. How God understood our nature that He would plan so perfectly for us - freedom and protection - the rhythm of our soul's journey.

January 2nd

Sunrise

How amazingly "warm" for January – no snow and mild. It amazes me how I never tire of looking for the ducks and braving the cold in my housecoat to go and throw seed for them. I marvel at every sunrise, whether it is a thin line on the horizon weighed down by dark and stormy sky or so brilliantly red you'd deny it in a painting.

It amazes me and humbles me to know how God never tires of watching over us. He waits and watches and hopes that we'll see him. How he longs to transform our hesitation, our doubts, to heal our wounds and address our fears.

Have you heard the seed splash in the water, have you seen it within your reach? He will not grab you or startle you. His patience is unfathomable, his concern for you is undiminishing.

"Look! Here I stand at the door and knock. If you hear me calling and open the door, I will come in, and we will share a meal as friends."
Revelation 3: 20

January 4th

God's Dawn

It is still incredibly mild for January. When winter closes in on the lake, as it surely will, all will become silent. Some mornings when the temperature has dropped below freezing, the water is still, a thin glassy surface of ice covering it. Crystals along the shore and over the rocks will melt as the sun rises.

The winter pair drifted by this morning when it was still mostly dark, the water a luminous still silver. As I stand on the shore watching tiny waves lap at the rocks and feel the gentlest of breezes I wonder - who am I? in this great space? -a tiny speck in God's creation, yet a part of the rhythm of life. It's hard to get up when it is still so dark but in the stillness I discover a certainty that I recognize I've always known. I think this is God's touch in our hearts - there before birth, before each new dawn. If you can run with the day and keep that still certainty in your heart, God's promise is with you.

Be still and know
that I am God.
Psalm 48: 10

How important it is to make time for stillness. For so many that time is non-existent and elusive. But how can you hear His voice without stopping to listen?

Discover what you already know, what He has already designed in you. Let God dawn in your life.

January 10th

Duck on the Rocks

The ducks were standing on the rocks this morning. Wind and snow swirled around our yard. I wanted to feed them but I had "winter inertia". They looked larger and more round – their feathers fluffed to keep them warm. I later walked down in my black winter coat before I went to work. Several were still in the shallows so I threw a handful of seed out to them. They don't like black – whether it's a sweater, a coat, a patterned bathing suit. Some ancient lesson of caution speaks to them.

Caution is a thoughtful assessment – instinctive in wildlife. Caution rouses our memories too – past hurts or fears or threats. I recognized their caution, I understood it. So I quietly backed away and left them to feed.

The Lord will never force you or pressure you. You can trust His call to you.

January 11th

Shelter

Jesus died to set us free, to give us a righteous life.

He will shelter Israel from the storm and the wind. He will refresh her as a river in the desert and as the cool shadow of a large rock in a hot and weary land.
Isaiah 32:2

Today is a stormy day. The waves are huge and constant, rolling over the rocks. Our flag is torn and snapping in the wind. Storms in life are constant and as unrelenting as the wind. As I sit watching out the window I didn't expect to see the ducks out there but sometimes they do come by, riding over the surge of waves. What is it that makes some venture out and others seek the safety and quiet of the willow branches by the creek?

Will you be wise and seek the shelter of our Lord or will you constantly be battered by the storms in your life?

January 12th

Flat Sky

I was watching the flat grey sky this morning. It was devoid of movement, of colour – drab and cold. A gull glided across my view and then another and another. They had been floating along the water's surface close to the thermal current. It reaches from the point across the bay and wavers out into the bay. In winter it becomes a high pressure ridge of ice and snow where warm water flows under the ice.

Life is still teeming below the drab flatness of the surface. I just can't see it.

God is still active in the world. He is like that current – supporting life, offering direction, always there beneath the surface of what we perceive as inactivity.

Even the desert will rejoice in those days. The desert will blossom with flowers and singing and joy.
Isaiah 35:1

January 16th

Crescent Moon

I awoke today to a thin crescent moon hovering just above the water. Tendrils of vapor wisp up into the air. There is the feeling of snow coming on the water. It has a quiet, ethereal feeling. The sleep of winter has come. The days of open water are limited. It's like saying good-bye to an old friend, and yet I know that spring will come and we will delight as if for the first time in the sunlight on rhythmic waves.

Our future is like that. Sometimes death is quiet and comes slowly and softly. Sometimes it is like a sudden storm, fierce and completely overwhelming. But hold fast, for a glorious newness of life is as certain as the sunrise. Isaiah 41:10 - Don't be afraid for I am with you. Do not be dismayed for I am your God. I will help you. I will uphold you with my victorious right hand.

January 17th
Howard's Pond

I saw an amazing thing yesterday. As I drove up our road past Howard's Pond, I watched as ten or twelve ducks flew over the treetops and seemed to hover, their wings tipping and wavering from side to side with the air currents. Suddenly they dropped with wings outstretched, through all the maple branches straight down like helicopters, to the pond's surface. I was amazed at their maneuverability. Normally they land long on the water with webbed feet outstretched before them.

Although the branches are an obstacle, they also protect the ducks from sudden attack. Obstacles and storms are so intertwined in life. But the rest and sustenance of the pond is still there. We all are aware of the potential of conflicts and obstacles but community is still there.

Seek first the kingdom of God.

January 21st

Antartic

The day I have been dreading has arrived. Yesterday was cold, crisp and sunny. The sky was so blue, the water sparkled. But clear, star-studded skies overnight meant that this morning the lake is still. Ice is covering it - as still and white as far as I can see.

A few years ago in the depth of winter, a film crew arrived on the ice. A movie was being made about an Antarctic research team. It was so interesting to see our beach and lakefront transformed with props and snow fans, even aircraft sections, into the staged reality of a place so incredibly far away.

Sometimes God seems like that - we stage some sort of reality, a collection of impressions and part truths and enter into the play of life. It gives the appearance of reality and yet something in us knows it is not complete. We are only complete in the fullness of the truth. Look to God's Word for that truth.

January 22nd

Hard Surfaces

Often I wake up in the dark and somehow my thinking has been made straight again. God's faithfulness and patience call out to the character he has given us. Even when I have stumbled, taken the wrong path and turned away from him, he is there. He renews my desire to live in accordance with his Will. The Holy Spirit stirs me to desire the obedience of right living.

We all at different times in our lives, will act as frozen as the lake - immovable and cold, rigid and hard-of-heart. Know that God stirs beneath the surface. Seek the openness of God and he will release you from the weight that imprisons you. He has promised that if you seek him, he will be found by you. His promise is faithful. His waiting is patient.

January 23rd

Ice Shifting

The ice has shifted, as it will for some time yet. It reminds me of pictures I've seen of tidal pools and estuaries where silt makes patterns between land and water. I can see small birds in the far distance flitting over the water – so much deeper and colder than close to shore. Will they stay to the very end, as the water surface gets smaller and smaller? What ancient timing will assert itself and signal that vast flight to warmth?

Are we prepared to acknowledge inborn wisdom and seek the path that has been laid out, given to us? Are we prepared to follow Christ's call and experience life-change through his great sacrifice for you, and me? We have been given the freedom to choose our own timing and destination.

Thank you Lord. What we perceive as a tenuous thread that connects us to you is in reality your promised hold of our souls.

O Lord our God, save us.
Gather us back from among the nations
So we can thank your holy name
And rejoice and praise you.
Psalm 106:47

Do not throw away this confident trust in the Lord, (God is mighty to save) no matter what happens.
Hebrews 10:35

January 25th

What is Faith?

I lay in bed this morning watching the sky awake with the sun. Pale grey low-lying clouds left a narrow band between the horizon and their weight. I watched as the undersides became tinged with red that silently spread out from the east. The red became tawny-pink and then peachy-yellow as the sun asserted itself. As the sun rose, the clouds became more transparent and I realized there were far more layers than I had first perceived. I could see movement and vapor and spaces of pale blue beyond.

The lake is silent and grey-white in it's frozenness. On the horizon is a narrow band of vapor - the last open water. What appears like big black rocks dotting the landscape are the shadows of ice sheets tipped up by the wind. The sun has climbed above the horizon and disappeared into the clouds. It has become a grey, winter day, the fleeting sunrise over.

Are we like this day? Do we perceive God's glorious newness of life and watch it dissipate into another grey day? How can we forget the moments of magic, of joy, of glimpses into eternity?

What is faith? It is the confident assurance that what we hope for is going to happen. It is the evidence of things we can not yet see.
Hebrews 11:1

God makes each day new. Walk in his assurance.

January 26th

Open Vistas

Open vistas always draw my attention - whether looking out over open water or at trees over distant farm fields. As winter approaches and birds start to mass for migration, it is always a wonder to see a flock flash up in the sky and fly in unison, swirling and moving in fluid motion across the openness. The shape of their collecting and the cohesiveness they display are one of nature's marvels. How can they choreograph such poetic flight? Can they feel it, delight in it?

God orchestrates the same connectedness in our lives. The pace may not be as rapid and soaring as the birds' but the patterns of interaction are just as definite. It is perhaps our view that is impeded, our sense of time misunderstood. One day we will look back and see the beautiful pattern our lives have been weaving.

So take a new grip on your tired hands and stand firm on your shaky legs. Mark out a straight path for your feet. Then those who follow you, though they are weak and lame, will not stumble and fall but will become strong.
Hebrews 12:12-13

January 27th
Corn Fields

Driving to the highway yesterday, as we were turning, we were amazed to see hundreds of ducks circling, landing, and moving through a cut-down cornfield. The lakes are frozen, it is the middle of winter and yet they are still here. Who is the leader and who are the followers? What wisdom or foolishness is holding them here?

If you are going to trust someone else with the quality of your life, make sure it is someone worth following. There is only one - blameless and spotless - Jesus. He will never cause you to stumble. He will accept your weakness. He will make all your paths straight.

February 2nd

Ice Groans

The ice groans and sends long shuddering vibrations for miles. I never really feel safe walking on it even though I know so well the contour and the depth beneath me. Yesterday I saw the first person trudging with a wood sleigh and ice-fishing gear. I at first thought he was walking out to the second pressure ridge but through the binoculars I realized he was walking this way - back to the beach. I wondered if in the time it took to focus the lens, he had changed his mind and was returning. Distance can be hard to gauge on the ice, it can be deceiving. What looks not far because there are no markers can be twice as far in reality. People have become disoriented when the shore is obscured and have gone in the wrong direction.

What are you letting be the markers in your life? Are you walking in the right direction? Do you have someone who will call you back if you become confused?

Though the Lord gave you adversity for food and affliction for drink, he will still be with you to teach you. You will see your teacher with your own eyes, and you will hear a voice say, "This is the way, turn around and walk here."
Isaiah 30: 20-21

February 3rd
Winter Moment

This is one of those quiet days when I am quite content to do nothing. The wind has sent long clouds across the sky and blowing snow off rooftops. The poor morning dove gripping the roof of the feeder gave up his solitary perch for the safety of the spruce tree. The movement of branches is the only sign of activity.

There is contentment in the moment, some hidden guilt that I should be more productive, a little yearning for spring still some time away, regret that time has passed that I may not have appreciated fully. I think God allows these small windows of time and place – his agenda has nothing to do with busyness and everything to do with our hearts.

February 6th
Frozen in Place

We expect and rely on the light of day to come. Do we even think of the air we breathe? It is as available and invisible as our heartbeat is certain. But, something has changed. The world's awareness has changed.

For my people have done two evil things – they have forsaken me – the foundation of living water. They have dug for themselves cracked cisterns that can hold no water at all!
Jeremiah 2:13

Will the need and desire to purify the land lead people to admit their wrong way of living and create a desire to be purified by God – the unchanging, enduring , faithful, waiting One.

"My wayward children," says the Lord, "come back to me, and I will heal your wayward hearts."
Jeremiah 4;22

Each morning I read God's Word and feel connected, immersed, strengthened by it. For this small time I feel whole. Then the day begins and the pressures of the world try to vaporize what I know to be true.
O Lord, strengthen me.

So get rid of all the filth and evil in your lives, and humbly accept the message God

has planted in your hearts, for it is strong enough to save your souls.
James 2:21

If you keep looking steadily into God's perfect law...
and if you do what it says...then God will bless you for doing it.
James 2:25

...we must care for orphans and widows...and refuse to let the world corrupt us.
James 2:27

The frozen lake is like a desert. So many people live in that same bleakness, looking to the horizon and seeing nothing redeeming, they see the bleak sameness of every day. But God can make the deserts bloom.

February 8th
Fresh Snow

Fresh snow, gently undulating over the landscape has a serenity, a purity - all the unevenness underneath it is covered by it. Our tracks and direction are clearly recorded as we make our way through the drifts. As children we would walk in each other's footprints or walk backwards trying to fool each other.

Our steps are so clearly seen by God. Is he seeing a random, erratic trail or are your steps measured and secure? Do you want him to see where you are going or are you on a path of deception?

February 16th

Spring Call

So then just as you received Christ Jesus as Lord, continue to live in Him, rooted and built-up in Him, strengthened in the faith as you were taught, and overflowing with thankfulness.
Col. 2:6-7

Yesterday while walking the dog in a numbing wind chill, the snow crunching underfoot, I heard a familiar bird call. It came from a tall spruce tree and aspen grove close to the road. I knew if I kept my eye on the spreading branches I would find it's source. To my absolute amazement a robin hopped from branch to branch. Such a familiar sound, such a familiar bird. I was astounded - and alarmed. How could it survive this hostile weather? What did it know that we did not? Could we dare to trust it's omen?

O that we might know the Lord. Let us press on to know him. For then he will respond to us as surely as the arrival of dawn or the coming of rains in early spring.
Hosea 6:3

Hope and spring, God's call to our hearts!

February 19th

New Day

This is the day the Lord has made. We will rejoice and be glad in it.
Psalm 118:24

The sky had a huge wind shear across it this morning - a huge dark diagonal cloud formation cut across the horizon. I am always fascinated by what God does through nature. Many people only feel his presence when nature acts out of character. They accept each day as nothing more than they're due. If only they would see God at work in their lives, each and every day, they would be humbled by His beauty, His great love for them. See something in your life today and think of it as a sign of God's care for you - whether it is the soft pink blush of the sky, or the sound of chirping as you walk out the door. Maybe it will be in a kind word that is unexpected.

Seek ye first the kingdom of God... Let God soften your heart and you will begin to see him - he will open your eyes to see and your ears to hear.

February 20th

Gentle Melt

The temperature has moderated. Overnight the air and snow have softened. A gentle melt is in the air. Even the atmosphere between ice and sky has a softer look. The light is flat so that the frozen lake is a monotone of white. Sometimes, I feel like that monotone. Neither incredibly inspired nor energized. We are so driven to perform and achieve.

A thought did grab me this morning - sanctuary. To me that is a place of rest and protection, of peace. In Ezekiel 11:16 the message from the Lord says - Although I have scattered you in the countries of the world, I will be a sanctuary to you during your time in exile...19: And I will give them singleness of heart and put a new spirit within them. I will take away their hearts of stone and give them tender hearts instead, so they will obey my laws and regulations.

Sometimes God's call to us IS gentle - let his soft contentment envelop your heart. This is his rest - a time to let the Holy Spirit transform your thoughts, to call you out of the desert into a newness of life. God will make the deserts bloom.

February 21st

Looking for God

If you look for me in earnest, you will find me when you seek me.
I will be found by you, says the Lord
Jeremiah 29:13

Give all your worries and cares to God, for he cares about what happens to you.
1 Peter5:7

In our society, giving our cares to God seems like passive abdication of our own responsibilities. It seems like the worst part of giving up - like surrender. Is this the great struggle of every generation - the struggle between recognition and opinion of this physical world and the recognition and surrender to our unseen God?

The natural world - the one I see through the ducks - works on a timetable established by the physical world, of seasons and climate, times of migration and breeding. Their survival depends on how well they adhere to and adapt to their physical world. This is God's great design for them. And yet, we are becoming aware that our lifestyles are compromising that rhythm - through pollution, loss of wetlands and climate change. What an interesting parallel. We have allowed so much of THIS world to divert our journey with God, to compromise the fullness of the life he has planned for us.

February 22nd

Walking on Ice

Two people are out on the lake, setting up to fish. They walked further out to drill their ice hole and are trudging back to pick up their gear. There is an aspect of unreality about seeing two dark figures on such a white landscape. How safe do they feel? Would they feel safe if the ice was as transparent as glass? Then they could see how far and deep they could fall. Maybe then their steps would be more measured for they would know the ice's thickness before they drilled.

So - what yardstick do you use to measure your steps? How transparent an outcome do you need in order to step forward? Our God calls us to step forward in faith.

What is faith? It is the confident assurance that what we hope for is going to happen. It is the evidence of things we cannot yet see.
Hebrews 11:1

Those two fishermen are anticipating a catch that they cannot yet see. If they don't catch it today, there is always tomorrow.

Let your day be like their's - full of God's promise. Anticipate his hand in your life. Be thankful in the waiting.

February 23rd
Hard Crust

The sun is brilliant on the snow this morning. Wind and freezing rain have polished surfaces and smoothed and rounded shapes. Our jetty stands out in shiny relief. As children we would so carefully walk on top of the snow, hoping our footsteps would not break through it's hard crust.

Events in our lives build up a hard crust in us too. So much of our energy is used in protecting and preserving that hard crust. We feel too vulnerable inside. Do you know the hardness and depth of that layer in your life?

God does send the wind and the rain, sculpting and perfecting. His desire is to break through that hardness in you, to touch that vulnerable heart within.

February 24th

Broken

Like many others in our neighborhood, we had to remove the heavy snow load from our roof. Using a wide snow rake, we watched as mini-avalanches cascaded down and landed in a dry powdery poof around our house. It was hard on the boxwoods and hydrangea bushes. Only spring will reveal the damage. We have a large false astilbe at the corner of our kitchen window. It's branches are long and not well-supported. As I shoveled the snow away, I uncovered it's broken branches. The buds actually showed a hint of green. Two of those branches now sit in my kitchen window, the leafing buds a testimony to perseverance and survival.

Sometimes only careful observation will reveal to you the brokenness in someone else. Perhaps God is showing you, revealing an opportunity for you to do his work. Don't let that chance slide by. Take the time to lift someone who needs a hand. The rewards of encouragement are greater than you may think.

February 25th

Gentle Persistence

This time of year when the sun is getting warmer, if the wind is offshore, we can sit in our boathouse and pretend that it's summer. The sun is warm and welcoming in the shelter of frozen rocks and sand and last year's queen anne's lace. As I look out over the snow and ice I can hear water trickling. There are tiny holes in the ice. Water ebbs and flows out of them as the currents under the ice are always moving. It reminded me of the Columbia Ice Fields in the Rockies. These huge, ancient ice shields are being eroded by insistent water - one drop at a time. Water - such a simple element - with a force that can change the surface of the earth.

God is that force in our lives - his gentle persistence will wear away, skiff off and break down your exterior. But He is the Creator of all things. He has a plan for your life - a plan for good that will prosper you and give you a future. (Jeremiah29:11)

February 26th

Obedience

Today is one of those days when it feels like winter will never end. It is dull and windy. Our dog now has a snow-blown path down to the lake. The snow was so deep he could hardly struggle through it. He lifted his nose into the wind and his ears perked up. I could see his excitement at whatever scent he caught in the air. He tried to jump through the deep snow to follow it and it took many calls to get him to turn around and come in.

What did he smell and recognize? What memory did it trigger? How willing he was to struggle through the snow to go exploring. I could see he was torn between following the scent and obeying me. In the end, cookies won out - the reward for returning.

As Christians, how easily we are enticed away from our true course. How exciting the unknown adventure, how tantalizing the call to explore. Obedience is often seen as dull, repetitive and predictable. When you know the path you should be on, recognize temptation for what it is - an attempt to divert you from commitments, from the one you have chosen to follow, from the one who chose you and called you by name.

February 27th

Mom's Dawn

Heard a song this morning - "You are never walking alone. There is someone calling you by name." How uplifting it was.

Five years ago this morning, early in the darkness, my mother died. She had diminished before our eyes. Her tiny frame just seemed to fade away, her breathing softer and softer until there was no more. We would talk to her, knowing that hearing was the last function to go. I remember saying - Hey, Mom - knowing I could not even say that much longer. She had said her good-byes days before. There was a peacefulness to her leaving - a quietness that to this day I can feel. Her faith was certain even though she never could explain it. She just lived it. No condemnation, no idle gossip, a certainty of goodness in most things.

On coming home that early day, the pre-dawn sky was the most glorious and beautiful pink wash across the whole horizon. It was grand, and gentle, and serene. How uplifting it was. There was someone calling her by name.

O that we might know the Lord. Let us press on to know him. Then he will respond to us as surely as the arrival of dawn or the coming of rains in early spring.
Hosea 6:3

February 28th

Mountains and Valleys

"Here I am again - in need of resurrection. You can make me whole again."

Yesterday morning was a mountaintop for me. It was full - full of sweet sadness, gratefulness, and certainty. Being "gripped by the greatness of God" is a singular thing in that it compares to nothing else. In Christian writing, the mountain peaks and valleys are symbols of our walk - sometimes lofty, many times lowly and alone. That God presides over all things can be crystal clear one day and totally obscured on others. His faithfulness is constant, his wisdom is beyond our scope of knowing. How easily we forget the mountain top when we are wandering on the flat plains of everyday life. Such is our human nature. On those days when there is nothing on the horizon that has not stretched out behind you for days, know that he is still the wise One, watching over you.

March 1st

Torn

God did not send his Son into the world to condemn it, but to save it.
John 3:17

We had every intention in the fall of taking down our Canadian flag. Then the rains and changing weather sent us indoors. It was usually in the wind and rain that I would look out and regret not taking it down. It is torn and dirty now but it still flies and gives us the wind's direction and strength. We will replace it with a new one - fresh and clean and bright against the sky.

You already know that God is like that. No matter how torn and worn you are, he will make all things new. It seems we are most aware of God in our own shortcomings, in our times of doubt, when the world is demanding more than we have. You are worth more to him even in your torn state than all the riches of this world.

And the one sitting on the throne said, "Look, I am making all things new!" And then he said to me, "Write this down, for what I tell you is trustworthy and true."
Revelation 21:5

March 5th

God's Word

Turn my eyes from worthless things, and give me life through your word.
Psalm 119:37

The sky was dreary today – hardly any definition between dull snow and flat sky. It was hard to see the horizon. Some days it IS hard to see beyond the same-ness of those long winter hours. Our lives are like that too – we keep repeating the same mistakes, the same uncompromising position with others. Time and again we wonder at the reasons for life, our emptiness acutely felt. Do we look for fulfillment in the wrong things, in all the wrong places as the song says?

God's Word can be like sunlight as it washes over the ice and snow – creating depth and shadows and illuminating all the details of footsteps, snowmobile tracks and wispy clouds in the sky. It can change your perspective in an instant.

Someone once sent me an email that Psalm 119 is the actual centre of the Bible and the longest Psalm.

Your word is a lamp for my feet
And a light for my path.
Psalm 119:105

March 7th

The Path

We have blown a path down to the boathouse – more times than we would like. The dog walks down it to sniff the air over the lake. It is higher than his back – like a dog-size cliff wall of snow. Today he thought he could jump up and walk over the hard surface. He sank down after a few steps. I thought I was going to have to put on my boots and go down and dig him out. He just sat there – suspended in snow. I called to encourage him and he struggled out, limping back to the door. It made me sad to see him limp with age but I love him even more when I see that joyful spirit in spite of his weakness.

Do not think for a moment that God is waiting for you to perform at a certain level before you come to him. I think he limps and struggles with each of us, loving us in all our weakness. Be encouraged, even if the snow feels impassable. How gently and sweetly he waits for you – calling you by name.

"I will lift my eyes to the Healer – of the hurt I hold inside. I will lift my eyes to the Maker... " by Casting Crowns.

March 8th

Bogged Down

I could see someone way out on the ice this morning. Using my binoculars I could see two people with an ATV. It was bogged down and they were digging around it to free it from it's pitched position. They will be exhausted by the time they dig it out.

Sometimes we get bogged down even when we feel prepared and equipped for a planned excursion. God has given us his Word for those times when we get bogged down in this world. His word will strengthen us when we are weak and exhausted. It gives us the tools - knowledge and wisdom - to set us on the right path, again and again.

Your commands make me wiser than my enemies,
for your commands are my constant guide.
Psalm 119:98

How sweet are your words to my taste; they are sweeter than honey. Your commandments give me understanding; No wonder I hate every false way of life.
Psalm 119:103

March 10th

Power

For God has not given us a spirit of fear and timidity, but of power, love, and self-discipline. So you must never be ashamed to tell others about our Lord.
2Timothy 5:7

When we allow others to intimidate us and our faith, we lose the effectiveness of the message. When God stands beside me, who can come against me? Ask God to convict you of his strength, the truth of the Gospels. Ask for His power in your life. Loving an "enemy" - someone in opposition to you - does not mean accepting their opinion of you or allowing them to control you. It means seeing that they are also created in God's image. He has great plans for them as He does for you. Pray that they will become aware of Him, that He would direct their steps, that He would open their eyes to see.

Do not stand still and watch as someone robs you of what is yours - the peace of the Almighty.

March 13th

God's Hand

You will receive power when the Holy Spirit comes on you.

We equate power with popularity, recognition or great wealth. The power of the Holy Spirit comes to those with faith and conviction. It transcends our weakness and imperfection. It is that aspect that lets us soar like eagles, even at times of confusion around us. God is like that - He can lift us up when we most need a clear view of His grace, his understanding of our pain. At times our greatest victories come when we separate worldly worries and accept the grace and hand of God in our small affairs.

I am thankful that His great mercies are new each day (Lamentations 3:22) I may have fallen, over and over - but still He cares enough to help me up - again.

March 14th

My Own Voice

This morning is hazy - the ice has gotten heavy and grey looking. Pools of water are appearing on it's surface. The ice will continue to get heavier, will begin to move and break up. Eventually it will sink to the bottom and the lake will be active once again.

Has God begun to work in your life? Sometimes we feel the weight of His truths in our thoughts. How he nudges us to correct those things that are not good for us. Forgive me for speaking out-of-turn, for not acknowledging your wisdom and kindness, for using my own voice when it is yours I need to hear.

Teach me your ways O Lord, that I may honor you.

March 16th

Trickling Water

The sound of water trickling down the eaves and dripping from the tree branches greeted me this morning. What pleasure to stand out on the step feeling the damp fresh air. As I sat looking out the window, I realized the first duck was waddling over the ice and water near our jetty. My first impulse was to take some seed down and throw it over the open water near the boathouse. But as I thought about it I realized that was my own need. This duck had been well-fed all winter at Howard's Pond. Iwas quite content to simply watch his progress over the ice.

How much of the good we do for others is a selfless act of care, how much for our own desire for usefulness?

March 27th

Gulf of Mexico

Son of man, you live among rebels who could see the truth if they wanted to, but they don't want to. They could hear me if they would listen, but they won't listen because they are rebellious.
Ezekiel 12:1-2

This is so much like our times, and the many generations before us. Are we more rebellious than our parent's parents?

While out on a catamaran in the Gulf of Mexico, I was so aware of my own insignificance - of age, and diminishing strength; I was struggling with seeing all my flaws. Everyone seemed young and so carefree. I felt weighed down by doubts and envy. I glanced at a young couple and was drawn to the tattoo on his upper arm. "The Lord is my mighty fortress. He is my rock and my refuge. For the honour of your name, lead me out of this peril...I entrust my spirit into your hand. Rescue me, Lord, for you are a faithful God. Psalm 31: 3-5

It's effect on me was like Jesus instantly calming the

stormy waves - peace and ease flowed over me. I was not insignificant. The Lord watches over every one of us. He is mighty to save. Tears welled up as I realized how he touched me so far from home.

The power of scripture is so strong; if people would only know and accept it. I thanked him for his tattoo, wondering if he had been in the Forces in the Middle East. How many others like me will be affected in seeing such a young, honorable person wearing his faith so visibly for all to see.

The Lord does move through his people, calling them, strengthening them.

So be strong and take courage
All you who put your hope in the Lord!
Psalm 31:24

April 2nd
Struggling

The world's sin is unbelief in me.
John 16:9

I wonder if my inability to write is more to do with God waiting for me to listen to Him and less to do with spring's coming being stalled - somewhere.

The ice is receding along the shore. How reflective the water is! The blue of the sky shines in it's stillness. How I long for the waves to break up the flat expanse of ice.

Is that how God uses the "waves" in our lives? To break up the resistance in our hearts? It is hard for us to see opportunity in our struggles. We try to simply get through them to the best of our ability. Do you believe that your burdens would be lighter if you sought out the Lord, if you knew He walked along side of you through your days?

The world's sin is unbelief in me.

How the Lord longs for you to know him, to see him in all your circumstances. Ask him to show you His presence. Be willing to see His reflection. He will show up in the simplest of moments, in the stillness of your heart.

April 3rd

Spring's Stall

It is so cold today even the bare branches look stiff and frozen. It amazes me to see vapour wisping up from the dead grapevine that climbed over the rocks last summer. Even in all this cold the sun is warming these rocks. Such a clear analogy – that the light of God can penetrate something as inert and immovable as rocks and warm them to a response. In what circumstances are you as inert and immovable? Do not deceive yourself into believing the Lord does not see and understand your stubborness, your unyielding heart. Let Him be your rock.

Rescue me, for you always do what is right.
Bend down and listen to me;
rescue me quickly.
Be for me a great rock of safety,
a fortress where my enemies cannot reach me.
Psalm 31:3

April 4th

Rocks

I was wandering around outside yesterday, enjoying the flat grass, the absence of drifts of snow and the accumulated hardened footprints of winter. I became aware of how many small piles of rocks were left strewn around from last summer – by the dock, by the planter on the boathouse, at the back door. I can remember the hot, hazy summer days when I had time to putter in the water, selecting and rejecting rocks along the shore. How ancient and timeless they are. This was once a great glacial lake, its shores miles away. Time has eroded and worn huge boulders, crushed them and left all these small ones, moved along by water, wind, and ice.

The Old testament is full of times of God's great events and the people's response in building monuments of rock and stone – in acknowledgement of His speaking into their lives.

The next morning he got up very early. He took the stone he had used as a pillow and set it upright as a memorial pillar. Then he poured olive oil over it.
Genesis 29:18

April 5th
Easter Lily

Today I received an Easter lily. It came as a gift from a new friend. It, like spring daffodils has a trumpet-like flower - herald of spring and of new life beginning. In Christian life it has come to symbolize the Resurrection. It's white petals open wide, almost like the Lord's arms - thrown wide to embrace us all, to draw us to him. He calls- Here I am. Come to me for I have chosen you. Rejoice, all of you who put your trust in the Lord.

You will show me the way of life,Granting me the joy of your presence and the pleasures of living with you forever.
Psalm 16:11

April 7th

Open Water!

But I have stilled and quieted myself, Just as a small child is quiet with its mother. Yes, like a small child is my soul within me.
Psalm 131:2

Contentment is an enormous gift from God. The lake in front of me started to open up yesterday. Rain, more than sunshine hastens the process of melting. The wind sent tiny ripples over its surface. I had forgotten how much movement there is in open water. This morning it is frozen again. I know it won't be long before the sound of waves will be an everyday thing. But today I am content to slip back into winter's routine. The fire is warm and I am thankful and secure watching snowflakes drift past my window. I am content knowing the tulips and hyacinths are waiting - for the warmth of the sun is returning.

Rest in the certainty of God's knowledge of you. Wait patiently for His gifts for your life. Be still and thankful for what He has already given you.

April 9th

Trust

You know what I long for, Lord;
You hear my every sigh.
Psalm 38:9

Jesus stood silent before his final accusers. He knew God's plan. God is so steadfast and faithful. He is completely trustworthy. Can you completely trust those around you? When you feel you have been wrongly accused, ask for the Lord's wisdom and understanding. He hears your every sigh. This world is not the conclusion. God's eternal wisdom will provide for you. Trust his judgment and his help in times of upheaval. Trust in his Word and look to it for answers. He will speak to you through its pages and its stories.

This is what is meant by - Cast your cares upon the Lord. Anyone can believe God's promises when all is going well. It takes faith to believe when your problems are mounting and no answer has come. Wait - for he is steadfast and faithful. He is completely trustworthy.

April 11th
Sounding Ice

Last night the lake started to sound. It sounded like a jet going overhead but it never faded in the distance. It reminded me of swinging a skipping rope over my head to hear the swoop of air, round and round. It awoke me through the night, its moaning very loud. Our flag was limp and silent. No wind was causing the movement. This morning the ice is still and silent. Standing at its edge, I can hear faint crinkles and pings like fragile glass breaking everywhere. It seems still and smooth.

Our exteriors are often the same - smooth and serene, while all kinds of emotions are rumbling through our thoughts. Life's pressures cause ongoing cracks - mocking, slander, anger and jealousy. Worthlessness and shame lie deeply hidden. The holiness God planted deep in our hearts gets dishonored.

Then I will sprinkle clean water on you, and you will be clean. Your filth will be washed away, and you will no longer worship idols. And I will give you a new heart and new and right desires, and I will put a new spirit within you. I will take away your stony heart and give you a new obedient heart.
Ezekiel 36:25-26

The Lord is always ready to hear our prayers and bless our requests. When our thinking is made right, our hearts are more pure. Our prayers are more in line with God's heart. Ezekiel 36...35 And when I bring you back, the people will say, This God-forsaken land is now like Eden's garden.

God is so willing to breathe peace into your heart but you must make room for him. He will show you things you thought you had dealt with and hidden away. Sometimes the rumbling will be long, shuddering through your heart. Sometimes, He will take your fragile thoughts and show you the flaws in your thinking.

Make room for the Lord to work in your heart. What was once God-forsaken will become like a spring garden - fragrant and hopeful and honorable - the way he intended for you to live.

April 14th
Open Vista

I have been busy and distracted this week. What I have longed for for weeks has happened without me! The lake is open, the undulating waves are rhythmic and soothing. One day I took some photos of the ice coming and going, breaking up and compacting again. All this transpired as it has for years and years, our life situations of no consequence.

We often see everything around us like that – we are of no consequence; the rhythms of life ebb and flow and we have no impact on it, invisible.

God has a purpose and a timetable for our lives that we may not recognize – until one day, we realize the ice is gone and the vista opens up before us.

The moving ice has strength and power that is hard to fathom. Huge boulders have been lifted and rolled, as if effortlessly. Will they fall back in place when the ice has disappeared or will they be part of the new landscape?

April 23rd

Swallow

The swallows were swooping and diving this morning - each claiming the bird houses by the shore. What determines which one will take up residence? Does the strongest and most determined prevail or is it a game of chance, one willing to enter and sit waiting for a mate to relieve it's perch? Once the eggs are laid, one is always on guard - sometimes on top of the house, waiting for the return of the other so it can take off. How they enjoy the sun and air currents - so invisible to us but so in tune with their senses!

If only we could be as confident that every day God will provide for us just what we need. There would be no rush to be first in line. Anxiety would be replaced by trust and real expectation. We would learn the wisdom of knowing the difference between need, and want. We would understand the lessons of waiting, of when to take a stand for things that really count. We would know that God will provide for us the way He has provided for nature.

April 26th
Loon's Call

Last night was still and cool, the lake like cool glass, no moonlight rippled on it's surface. About 4 a.m. the loons started calling. There is no knowing how far out on the lake they are. I remembered hearing them before - one calls out in the distance and from far far away another answers the call. Their haunting voices are locating each other, keeping track of their positions. Loons are fairly solitary, even when together they swim and dive apart.

I think our fascination with them is the sense of aloneness and wilderness they represent. They seem an ancient species, untouched by our modern lifestyle. Do we look to them for some understanding of their strength, some elusive simplicity that echoes in our hearts, some memory of truth and clarity? Perhaps we would like to know that when we call out in the darkness, God will answer our call. Such companionship, such a certainty that he will hear your call.

April 30th

Merganser's Romance

For a week or more a pair of mergansers have been "romancing" off our shore and sunning themselves in the early morning on the rocks nearby. Their appearance is startling – the female with a striking crest of feathers and the breeding male a bold black and white. Their piercing eyes see beneath the clear water, waiting for minnows. I realized I was almost overlooking their poetic nature because I was watching and waiting for momma to show up. Last year she arrived on April 17. I have walked down our sidewalk many times with seed in hand hoping she would be quietly waiting in the shallows. How empty the lake has seemed.

May 10th

Alarm

The lake was very noisy last night. The geese were constantly honking; they seemed very unsettled. About 3 a.m. they set up the most constant alarm, sounding their literal "honk" in bold unison. I wondered whether the mink hunts at night. Even this morning the lake is noisy and unsettled. The upstart mergansers have taken over the rocks near our jetty. I hear the ducks flying overhead, their wings wobbling as they look for a different place to land. There has been a rebellion of sorts - the mergansers are holding position and the ducks are displaced.

Are you in a place like that? Is something or someone blocking your path? Are you feeling forced to be somewhere unfamiliar? Is something in your heart sending out an alarm?

Hold on to the one who is unshakeable. He is your sure footing. Let that certainty sink into your soul. Sometimes we don't see the Lord at work until the danger has passed and we have time to look around us. Praise the one who is forever faithful.

May 14th

God's Presence

I picked the first spring flowers in the garden last night – purple hyacinth, narcissus, forsythia and tulips. The intense fragrance of their bouquet was intoxicating.

Following God can be as intense and even more intoxicating but sometimes a gentle, elusive scent can call us just as strongly into His presence. Every small and simple flower is like a beacon of hope, a whispered promise of the Lord – I am here among you.

May 15th

Young Ducks

New young ducks were paddling along this afternoon - a very still and humid day. Thunderstorms will probably gather again tonight. I threw seed out for them - a small amount really - and they stopped to nibble at it. They seemed unaware that I was standing there, oblivious to the hand that threw the seed. We are many times just like these two. We think things that work out in our favour just happened or we got lucky. We give no more thought to the Giver than these ducks did. They float along on clear water, the algae on the rocks exactly what the ducklings will need to feed on in a few weeks, the sun warming the rocks and encouraging it's growth.

I found it oddly sad that there was no recognition, no excitement at finding seed floating before them. I felt no attachment to them, no promise of their return tomorrow. How many times are we just like that to the One who blesses us? The One who watches over us and provides so much more than we recognize?

May 16th

Indigo Bunting

Out trees are teeming with birds. They flit and flutter through the softly swinging branches of the spruce trees. Yesterday I saw my first indigo bunting, sitting in our feeder waiting out the downpour. His color was even more intense in the stormy darkness. He was like a jewel in the garden. I would doubt that a single feather would be that saturated deep teal color - the layering of feathers intensifies his appearance.

The beauty in our lives is like that too. The layering of experience, of trials and tribulation, shapes us and colors our view of life.

Will you allow God's call to shape your world? Be prepared for colors you have never seen, for experiences only He can orchestrate. Open your eyes to see and your heart to recognize Him.

And I heard how many were marked with the seal of God.
Rev.7:4

May 18th
In the Beginning

In the beginning God created the heavens and the earth...3: Then God said, "Let there be light and there was light... and God saw that it was good.
Genesis 1:3

Thank you Lord, for all the good things of this world, for everything that is good is from You. Thank you Lord that you redeem us, for redeeming us from all our failures, all our fears. As we make our plans and dream our dreams, thank you for guiding us.

...your promises are backed, By all the honor of your name.
When I pray, you answer me;You encourage me by giving me the strength I need.
Psalm 138:2,3

Search me, O God, and know my heart; Test me and know my thoughts.
Point out anything in me that offends you,
And lead me along the path of everlasting life.
Psalm 139:23,24

May all your steps be sure, your direction the one God's given you. May your actions reflect His honor and lead others to want to know Him.

Help us to walk in your shadow, that all light shines on You - for it is not about us Lord, but your Spirit within us.

Then God said, "Let there be light and there was light. And God saw that is was good.

May 19th

Dinty and Babies

A few days ago , on May 17, in the evening Bob called me outside – "Your duck is here". Why should I be so excited about a duck? It is only one of too many to count, on lakes all over the country. I realized that for me it was a sign of God's faithfulness – my faithful watch and God's faithful provision. As I looked at this duck , I wanted her to be momma but I knew it wasn't. She has two tiny ducklings – probably two days old – soft, golden feather down bobbing on the water. It wasn't until she turned to swim away that I saw the back of her head and recognized her – Dinty momma from last year, with the soft pink mouth and tiny voice. There was no hesitation in her approach this year. We will see if the babies will eat out of my hand. New for her, a male accompanies them. He stands watch as the family feeds in the shallows.

Do you see how God has blessed your life? Do you recognize those who wait for you, those who stand watch for you? Be thankful for His provision. Is He calling you to be watchful for someone else, to be a blessing in their life?

May 20th
Two Days Old

Dinty's two-day old ducklings:

May 21st

Whom Do You Call

In times of want, in times of plenty
On whom do you call?
Do you search yourself or give no thought
To the answer of eternity?

Do you know with certainty
The God who made you, calls you?
Have you searched for Him and found
His certain answer in your soul?

On what do you rest your reputation–
What is it that defines you?
Is it truth and honesty and justice,
Is it care, concern, and willingness to do?
Then you know the Lord Almighty,
For He resides in you.

May 22nd

Searching

The time is surely coming," says the Sovereign Lord, "when I will send a famine on the land - not a famine of bread or water but of hearing the words of the Lord.
Amos 8:11-13

People will stagger everywhere from sea to sea, searching for the word of the Lord, running here and going there, but they will not find it. Beautiful girls and fine young men will grow faint and weary, thirsting for the Lord's Word.

Childhood Summers

Today I ventured into the ice cold water in hopes of enticing Dinty to eat from my hand. It was so cold my feet were cramping. Both she and the male came within a foot of me but backed off when I stepped into the water – too close for comfort. I was surprised that she would dive, her open beak gobbling seed off the sandy bottom. She must feel safe enough with me being the watchman. Tomorrow is another day. Being patient is part of the process. Without patience there would be no chance of feeling tiny suede-soft feet jumping from my hand. Patience is worth the reward.

How patiently God has watched and waited through generations of family. I sometimes wish I had been old enough to hear my grandmother's wisdom – raising six children in the 1920s.We always saw them in summer – at a large summer home on Lake Erie. There were always raspberries and blueberries from their bushes sitting in open bowls in the refrigerator. A large cottage green jug held old-fashioned lemonade.

These were the only times I saw my cousins as most of my aunts and uncle chose to live in the U.S. I was never aware of the family dynamics at work until many years later my mother confessed to all the stress she felt over rivalry and the " behavedness" of us all. The master bedroom that my parents shared was really the second floor verandah. It had the best view over the treetops and first thing in the morning we would open up the old French doors and jump into their bed, the wood floor cool on bare feet. We could tell by the temperature, the wind blowing through the trees and the sound of the surf, whether it was a sweater or bathing suit day.

It was a rare time of all the family having lunch together – often on the beach. With fifty-seven steps to the beach, my mother hated forgetting anything. Lunch was packed in two old cookie tins - sandwiches and cookies, grapes and apples. My parents would sit on towels while we played and jumped in the waves. I never gave a thought to what they talked about. They were just there, solid and sure. I later knew of my father's anxiety of being passed over for a promotion, and my mother's desire to work in a time when most stayed home raising children.

My grandfather was larger than life - even coming daily to the beach in the cool of late afternoon - in grey flannels and a navy blazer, his camera bag over his shoulder. I remember wondering how he could stand socks and good black shoes in the sand. He took pictures of us and laughed at our antics. It was his desire that brought all of us together, his satisfaction in bringing us to the cottage. I believe his family was his blessing.

I know my grandmother cared for us but she was somewhat distant. It was from her I got my artistic sense - she always had fresh flowers and beautiful fringed pillows on her sofa. She played the grand piano that resided in their sitting room. I don't remember any offer at letting us play it. I got my impatience with those less than perfect from her too. She hated it when my grandfather would encourage us to eat our Sunday noon dinner peas lined up on our knives. I'm sure that's why he did that - just to ruffle her feathers, keep her humanly involved. She very quietly left peppermint patties and fruit-covered jellies in a box in her sideboard. How clever we thought we were at sneaking them.

I could describe their house in great detail - something about it's solidness and order penetrated my very thinking. To this day I can visit someone else's home and immediately know that sense of purpose, of order, of respect for family, of mutual need and support - of peace, perhaps. I do not recall any turmoil, only gentle teasing. How blessed we were, too young to understand it and appreciate it.

I'm sure we kept them young, from getting too set in their ways. My grandfather had an old black Packard, the seats upholstered in wool that picked and scratched young legs in shorts. He would drive us very sedately to the downtown Kresge's and laugh at us gleefully choosing inflatable tubes made like ducks and sand pails and sifters for the beach. It was pure extravagance to us - as were store-bought cookies and cream soda.

All of my four aunts and an uncle graduated from university. The sadness and failures in their lives were never discussed until my own father had passed away. How much stronger we might have been if it had been allowed to admit weakness, to ask for advice, to simply cry when the world was being unfair. We were not allowed to dwell on ourselves so we felt immense guilt over our own indecisiveness, our own anxiety over everyday affairs. But it made us strong too, and independent – certain spouses would call it "stubbornness". It made it harder for God to scale the walls and break down barriers and open doors to our souls.

Oh, but He is patient – the reward is worth His patience. We are all His family, He is our heavenly Father. He has prepared a wonderful mansion for us, full of jewels and fruit jellies, of truth and respect, of mutual love – of peace.

May 23rd

His Light

After yesterday's brilliant sunshine, today's overcast sky is very somber. What a difference the sun makes to our mood, our outlook on the day. Jesus said, "I am the light of the world." His light is constant, it is the beacon of hope in the darkness of our struggles. So seek the light!

May His face shine upon you and give you peace.

Your word is a lamp for my feet
And a light for my path.
Psalm 119:105

May 24th

Geese on the Lawn

Yesterday, after coming home from an exhausting workday, I realized the geese had spent the day on our lawn. They are so messy! I was annoyed at the thought of spending an hour cleaning up after them. It spoiled my enjoyment of the evening. What should have been my time of rest and thankfulness for my surroundings was supplanted by an unpleasant chore. I allowed pleasure to be robbed from me. This is how the Deceiver likes to see us - so distracted by small things that we take our eyes off God's blessings.

A man's heart plans his way,
But the Lord directs his steps.
Proverbs 16:9

When you allow yourself to sit quietly and read God's Word, you will begin to hear Him - sometimes gently and with great love - as I did looking out over the water, realizing how beautifully and thoughtfully He created our world. How small a time it will take to clean up the yard - and sometimes, you will hear Him with reproof and chastening - stop focusing on distractions and letting them steal your peace.

Allow yourself to experience God's grace, choose to let Him direct your life.

May 28th

Mink on the Rocks

Twice in the last week I have come almost face-to-face with the mink - without my camera! The first time I was sitting by the dock feeding the young males. No alarm was sounded by them. I was amazed to see the mink swimming right under me, an apple core in it's mouth. The second time while mounting our purple martin house, he came over the rocks not two feet from me. Again I was amazed - by the rock bass he had in his mouth. It was almost the same size as the mink. What strength his jaws must have to carry that weight, what deadly quick reflexes it must have to snatch it's prey.

Although I marvel at his self-reliance, and his elusive behavior, I have no affection for him. He is the size of a large squirrel, his shiny coat a dark brown. He fulfills his place in the order of nature. I think what bothers me is how oblivious he is to anything other than his own needs. He is self-reliant and seemingly solitary.

We too can be oblivious when we determine to do or get for ourselves without thought to the effect on others, without determining or knowing what is right.

I reach out for you.
I thirst for you as parched land thirsts for rain.
Show me where to walk,
For I have come to you in prayer.
Psalm 143:6

May 29th
Cedar Hedge

This is a perfect morning. The sun on the water sends ripples of reflection over the cedar hedge. The air is bright and clear. The birds are nesting and I can hear the call of tiny voices in the hedge.

All God's ways are perfect. Don't you want to know your place in His perfect plan? He wants to lift you up on wings like eagles. Let your soul dance in the new dawn, eager for life, joyful in His care for you.

O people, the Lord has already told you what is good, and this is what he requires: to do what is right, to love mercy, and to walk humbly with your God.
Micah 6:8

May 30th

Dinty's Young

In the early evening, as sun lowering turns everything golden, a truce is achieved on the rocks. Standing, preening, or sleeping, the geese, mer-gansers and the ducks all share the last warm rays of sun.

Feeding Dinty and her two offspring has become a bit dutiful. I watch with some annoyance as the male nips at the babies, downy tufts floating over the water. They can only get seed when he and Dinty are done. What test is that - that they learn to stay out of reach? That they learn a quick retreat? That they understand dominance and their lack of it? Dinty's young are always loners, swimming great distances away from her as if there was no connection between them. Momma on the other hand, scolded and protected and shepherded her seven until they were almost her own size. I am disappointed not to see her this spring. She was so responsive and delightful.

May 31st

Momma Returns

When you open your hand
You satisfy the hunger and
thirst of every living thing.
Psalm 145:16

While reading on this humid morning, I looked up to see a female duck on the lawn. I could have returned to my book but I am glad I went out with seed. As she approached me, I saw the familiar dark band through her eyes and stared in wonder at my "momma". She came right up to me on the sidewalk. If I could have stayed crouched down long enough I think she would have taken seed from my hand.

The Lord will satisfy your hunger, he will fill your heart with wonder and bless your faithful watch. He has called us to watch for his sheep - to feed those we encounter - to encourage their hearts and show them our God. Will you reach your hand out to someone in need? God will satisfy your thirst, and theirs.

June 1st

Babies Alone

Both babies were in the lagoon and responded to my call this morning. As they paddled over I wondered where the mother was? They shouldn't be alone. They dove for the seed on the sand, their tiny webbed feet like propellers on a motor-boat scooting them along the bottom. They are so buoyant, instantly popping to the surface. They have now developed miniature tail feathers that when fanned out act like small stabilizers on the undulating water. I watched them paddle around and wander back through the lagoon, never far from each other - two tiny ducks, alone but for each other - seemingly undaunted by the immensity of their environment. Maybe, for them the focus is on the moment, on the proximity of each other. They swam with ease, in unison with each other, their view of rocks and sand and ripples over the water, the sun warming them.

Would we all not like their simplicity? Their freedom and ease with their surroundings? - no huge expectations pressuring them, no race being declared, no judgment of their performance given? God can grant us that space, those moments of peace. He comes to encourage, not to condemn. He will supply for all our needs.

June 3rd
Gull and Mink Collide

This afternoon was hazy, humid and hot. As I lazily watched the "rock" community, thunder rumbled over the water. The sky was heavy and the air was almost oppressive. A storm watch had been posted. Many birds will scour for food before a storm and rough waves force them to safe places. The gulls were on the rocks, also many geese and male ducks. As I watched all the gulls lifted and circled, their squawking and erratic flying was unexpected. I saw one flapping his wings on the rocks, and then - I saw the mink. He dragged and bit the gull whose flapping wings became more sporadic. I could hardly believe it when the mink pulled it into the water. There was nothing I could do. Momma and the babies were still diving for seed on the sandy bottom. No amount of clapping and calling alerted her. I watched the mink tear and devour his catch. Would momma be next, or her young?

For all my noise and calling, momma was still unprotected and seemingly unaware. How many times has God called a warning, tried to raise our awareness, only for us to turn a deaf ear.

Where are the minks in your life? - the ones who prey on your weaknesses, who pull you down? Do you recognize the ones you can only be around when your defenses are strong?

June 4th
First Storm

Last night our first summer storm blew in. The winds whipped up waves that crashed over our jetty. It became dark so early in the evening, the sky an immense dark, rolling expanse. Storms, even though exciting, make me feel small. I have never been afraid of thunder and lightening, but living on the water has given me a new respect for the power of the wind. Such an invisible, uncontainable force. Only a fool would find himself out in a boat trying to outrun it. We see these regularly - those who have ignored all the warning signs of sky, temperature and changing cloud patterns.

God gives us the same warnings - in patterns of our lives, in the changing conditions of our hearts.

And I will destroy those who used to worship me but now no longer do. They no longer ask for the Lord's guidance or seek my blessings.
Zechariah 1:6

June 5th

Minnows

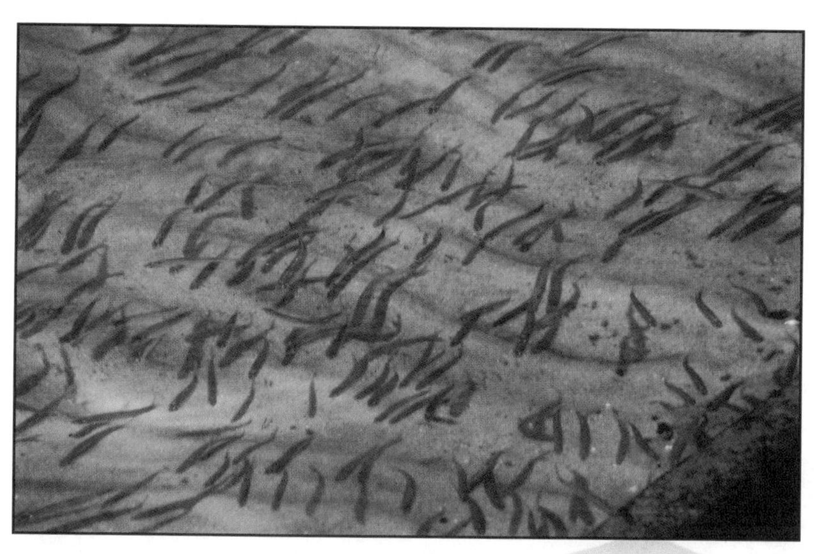

Standing on the dock, gazing into the water, a huge drift of minnows swam under me and swirled through the lagoon. There were literally hundreds, possibly thousands of them. It was amazing to see their formation and clear direction, their sandy colour and dark stripes a perfect camouflage. Only their movement drew my eye. God's abundance in nature, his perfect timing, humbles me. All of this happens without our knowledge or presence, yet it affects the very rhythm of our thinking. So God touches us – like a gentle caress in our thoughts, reminding us of his great provisions for us.

June 6th
Choppy

The lake is what is called "choppy" today. The waves are erratic in direction, white caps erupting everywhere. Many days, my own thoughts are in the same condition - going in too many directions, interrupted and noisy. That God created the wind that blows reminds me of prairie wheat fields whose grasses are waving in smooth unison, waves of green undulating in the sun. When we rigidly resist God's movement in us, we create the "chop" I see today.

June 11th

Baby Grackle

It seems every time I walk down the stone walkway, the ducks are following two steps behind me. They are under the feeder early in the morning and when dusk has faded. The two young have been left totally on their own. Yesterday, as I threw seed for them, the blackbirds were calling a warning. The young ones paddled out a safe distance and waited. The baby grackles were clinging to the tops of the cedar hedge waiting to be fed.

There is so much like this in our families today. Parents so consumed with their own work that children are left in the care of others, orphaned by the distractions of our material, demanding world. This is a time of such abundance - like the summer when life is pleasant and plentiful.

For I am planting seeds of peace and prosperity among you. The grapevines will be heavy with fruit. The earth will produce its crops and the sky will release the dew.
Zechariah 8:12

There is much to be done. We are called to continue God's work - in our homes, in our nation. Don't be lulled into thinking your work is done.

June 12th

Baby Swallows

The swallow's eggs have hatched as I hear tiny voices in the "apartment". How busy the parents are. How encouraging it has been to watch their faithful preparations and their joyous flight.

What are the times of anointing and refreshing in the Lord? Do all the birds that sing in the trees and flowers that bloom in the fields offer praise to God - in the way that He made them? Is this God's language of love - the trill and chatter of swallows and sparrows, the heavy fragrance of lilies blowing in the breeze? Is each new day an anointing of the Lord? Has He given you eyes to see and a voice to speak? Ask him to anoint your day.

Look at the birds. They don't need to plant or harvest or put food in barns because your heavenly Father feeds them. And you are far more valuable to him than they are. Can all your worries add a single moment to your life? Or course not.
Matthew 6:26-30

And why worry about your clothes? Look at the lilies and how they grow. They don't work or make their clothing, yet Solomon in all his glory was not dressed as beautifully as they are. And if God cares so wonderfully for flowers that are here today and gone tomorrow, won't he more surely care for you? You have so little faith!

June 13th

Ducklings on the Steps

I am still amazed the young will venture up our steps for seed left out on concrete. I find it unsettling that they are totally on their own. Yesterday they displayed their independence in chasing an adult male away. They charge with head down and great splashing to warn others away. How amazing, and how sad – that there is no loving, protective momma watching over them.

We are too often the same – struggling and asserting ourselves totally in our own strength, constantly watching for anyone getting too close. How proud and self- sufficient that makes us. Are you too proud to ask for help, to seek God's protective shade?

The Lord himself watches over you!
The lord stands beside you as your protective shade.
The sun will not hurt you by day,
Nor the moon at night.
The Lord keeps you from all evil and preserves your life.
The Lord keeps watch over you as you come and go,
Both know and forever.
Psalm 121:5-8

June 14th
Fireflies

Last night I saw the first fireflies of the season – their blinking glow almost a neon green in the dark. Who could ever question or deny the wisdom of our awesome Creator, the one who could think of such beautiful things and orchestrate their seasons? How profound is our God.

"Let not the wise man boast of his wisdom or the strong man of his strength or the rich man boast of his riches, but let him who boasts boast about this: that he (God) understands and knows me (you), that I am the Lord, who exercises kindness, justice and righteousness on earth, for in these I delight," declares the Lord.
Jeremiah 9:23-24

Sitting in the quiet evening light
I thank you for your gentle breath.
As I listen to your night sounds –
  the birds calling over the water,
  the robins in the cedar hedge.
I am amazed again by your
  generosity –and by your wisdom
In creating the myriad twinkling of
  fireflies– all echoes of your
  creation.

June 15th
Thoughts

All your thoughts towards me are holy.
Psalm 77:13

And the one sitting on the throne said, "Look, I am making all things new." And then he said to me, "Write this down, for what I tell you is trustworthy and true."
Revelation 21:5

The Lord's promises are pure, Like silver refined in a furnace, Purified seven times over.
Psalm 12:6

All he does is just and good, And all his commandments are trustworthy. They are forever true, To be obeyed faithfully and with integrity.
Psalm 111:7

Turn my eyes from worthless things, And give me life through your word.
Psalm 119:37

I rejoice in your word Like one who finds a great treasure.
Psalm 119:162

When all is confusion around you, trust in the truth of God's Word. These are for Hannah, Nicole and Cody.

June 17th

Mystery Solved

Yesterday the merganser babies fell (or jumped) from the overhanging birch tree into the lake. Fourteen young intently follow behind their mother attempting to climb onto her back. A mated pair will often roost ten to twelve feet high in a tree that is close to water. Now we understand why we were seeing them on our rocks each morning – feeding and resting, waiting for their young to hatch.

The mysteries of nature reveal to us the depth of God's creativity. God's ways are higher than our ways. All his plans are perfect.

Be strong today. Live your life with his purpose, his direction.

June 19th

Neglect

Where does neglect come from? One day we trust the Lord with our life, our family, our work, our inner self. Days come and go and disappointments and discouragement accumulates. With no real intent, we let God slide from our view. We forget that he is the very air we breathe, that he has placed wonders all around us. He loves us even in our pain and frustration. He may become silent in these times that we forget to honour him. It is a silence like a vacuum - where nothing thrives; not the silence of a peaceful place.

The Lord of all the earth waits expectantly - for you and me - to remember him with our faithful and thankful hearts.

Thank him today for the cool morning air that refreshes and ask again that he would show you his path. It leads to life - the one he has called you to live. He is calling you still. Will you answer?

You say, "It's too hard to serve the Lord," and you turn up your noses at his commands.
Malachi 1:13

June 20th

In Distress

"I am the Lord and I do not change...Now return to me and I will return to you," says the Lord Almighty.
Malachi 3:6

Last night we got a call from our neighbour who had found a baby merganser on the rocks by the shore. It was about four days old. This young one may have been injured when waves overcame it and pushed it into the rocks; it had been a stormy afternoon. The mother and the other young were nowhere to be seen and it was getting dark. His tiny, downy body and long webbed feet were just warm. He seemed less agitated when he was covered. I remembered seeing the mother on our rocks with her wings half-opened - like a shield or umbrella - with all her young trying to get close to her under her wings. We decided to release it in the morning; at night the mink or numerous cats would surely have found it. It would rally and chirp with its

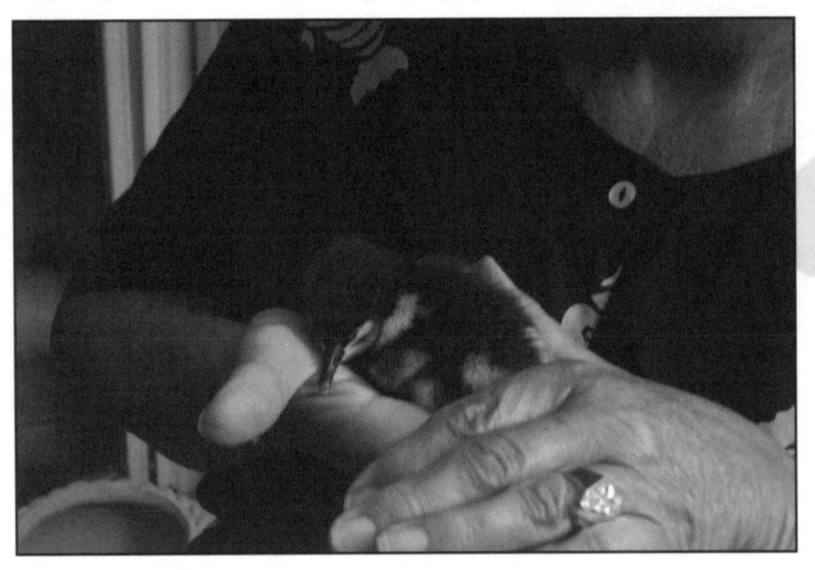

tiny voice. We made a nest with duck down and covered it. At five a.m. I woke, hoping to release it in the lake. A small, still form, to all account seemingly perfect, lay in the feather nest, cold to my touch. Such sadness enveloped me. His underside was pure white, his back spotted brown and white, almost like a fawn, its webbed feet long for such a small body. I wished I had left him in a rock crevice last night for then nature would have been his fate. I was the intruder into their pattern of life. I felt guilty.

God knows us. Even if our hearts condemn us, for he is greater than our hearts.

I will watch for the merganser family and count anxiously to see how many of her young survive.

The Lord never changes. He is the same forever. His council is always true – and hopeful. Death is so silent and cold. Who would choose death over life? Jesus died so we would have eternal life. It was his gift that we would not perish but live. John 3:16

June 21st

Poppa

The lake is teeming with new families. Momma's young from last year have young of their own. Two small ones were bold enough to challenge Poppa - and he conceded. The mother's coloring is a softer brown with golden, more open patterning in her markings. She arrived without hesitation, without fear but kept a respectable distance for awhile. She keeps her family close, just like Momma did. How does the Lord not play favorites?!

Poppa, the one lone, aggressive male, kept coming back. As I watched his display, I realized he was missing half his tail feathers. I looked at him and wondered what battle he had been engaged in, and with whom?

The Lord knows all our battles. His will is to heal all our wounds. Have you let him see your scars? Have you allowed him to speak into your heart?

June 23rd

Swallows First Flight

The swallows seem to have left. Two days ago they would dive at anything near the birdhouse. They flew and "clicked" at me not a foot from my head. They repeatedly dove at a young squirrel until they knocked him off the ledge he was sitting on. Now, all is silent. Did I miss the coming out and first flight?

June 26th

Momma

This morning Momma came at 6:30 with her three young. She watches my hand, knowing I will throw seed to her. As I progress down the steps, she comes closer. The black dab at the end of her beak and the dark streak through her eyes are so familiar to me. Later she settles her young on the flat rock and has come back to feed on the sandy bottom and will fly up on the jetty. How I know her moves!

God knows our moves like that. He watches over us and understands more than we think. His watch is sure and certain, his commitment to you is real. Look to his promises for hope.

June 27th

Summer

What is summer in the spiritual sense? It is the season of growing in the natural world - or reproduction of species, of fields of wheat and tall corn, of thunder and lightning, and fragrant winds. All things bask in warmth and strength. It is a season of physical activity rather than of introspection. Spring and fall are times of anticipation, of looking ahead; times when we easier lean on the Lord for direction. Summer is a season that draws us to our own strength perhaps, not God's provision. It is the easiest season to become part of the world and miss God's call. There is such abundance everywhere, we forget to be thankful for small things in the largeness of summer.

In what things are you so strong that God has no opportunity to shine in you? In what weakness have you learned to look to Him for support?

June 28th

Reunion

Yesterday was like a reunion of the clans. My original Momma and her three, her young now mommas with their own young, one of the orphans now in full mature colour, a new family and assorted males from Howard's Pond, were all milling around and squabbling. There was much splashing and displaying, and aggressive flapping of wings. It escalated into outright aggression. At one point, I thought Momma would be drowned. So many of her beautiful feathers floated away with the breeze – all the intricate patterns that clothe her, all soft and curved and beautiful. One of her young was just as aggressive, nipping and chasing No-tail-feathers, giving his tiny peeping call as he forced him farther away.

It reminded me of family reunions, where all come together for a summer barbeque, and a lot of sarcastic nips and posturing and discussions and disagreements surface. Where is the Lord in all of that?!

When you find you are defending yourself or your territory, remind yourself it all belongs to God. Wherever you stand, whatever you have, was His first.

"I promise you what I promised Moses: :Wherever you set foot,
you will be on land I have given you."
Joshua 1:3

June 30th

Merganser chicks

We saw a merganser family with nineteen chicks this morning. In the open water they were spread out, leaving a long rippling V behind each small chick. As they perceived our intrusion on the dock, instinct took over and they formed a tight line behind the mother and attempted to get on her back.

Wouldn't we all like that protection in the face of danger? How strong that mother was - swimming along with the weight of five or six on her back.

If God is truly in us, a part of our lives, when danger presents itself, we should, out of true closeness, seek His protective presence. Where do you flee? Is it truly strong enough to protect you?

I wait quietly before God,
For my hope is in him.
He alone is my rock and my salvation,
My fortress where I will not be shaken.
My salvation and my honour come from God alone.
He is my refuge, a rock where no enemy can reach me.
Psalm 62:5-7

July 2nd

Beauty in the Morning

As I sat in the early morning sun, purposely with eyes closed, I listened and felt the warm sun and the slightest of breezes. I heard the splashing and flapping of wings, the swoosh of feet diving. It was quiet and good. Seek those moments that God will give you, to restore your sense of his purposes in life. You can not hear him in the noise of life and he is infinitely worth listening to.

As I gazed at the ducks preening, and washing, and sipping cool water, I saw how beautiful it is to simply be what God intended. I saw how perfectly he designed them, how beautifully they fit into his plan. Know how beautiful you are, even in the day-to-day routine of life. Let others see your inner beauty - it will shine in you as you live God's everyday life- caring for children, walking with a friend, working and cooperating with others. Look and see yourself as God does, beautiful in the morning, worth every breath he gives you.

July 9th
Thunderstorm

Last night we had a surprise thunderstorm. It rolled in around dusk. Lightning flashed and thunder rolled for hours - lighting the sky like daylight. How much power it takes to light up the whole skyline like it's high noon! It was good to sit in wonder at the awesome display of power over the water, over the land and sky. When the wind and rain came - in sheets and howling - the tall spruce's branches waved frantically, the same ones we could hardly lift to trim the grass. How strong and invisible the wind is. The rain washed all the dust and dirt and old needles and maple wings from its branches. It was washed clean and new.

God does this for us too. He comes in unexpected storms, he surprises us with his strength, his focused energy. Allow him to bend your branches. Trust in his outcome. All is calm this morning, fresh and new in his sunlight.

"Anyone who listens to my teaching and obeys me is wise, like a person who builds a house on solid rock. Though the rain comes in torrents and the floodwaters rise and the wind beats against that house, it won't collapse, because it is built on rock. But anyone who hears my teaching and ignores it is foolish, like a person who builds a house on sand. When the rains and floods come and the winds beat against that house, it will fall with a mighty crash."
Matthew 7:24-27

July 11th

Gift of Vision

This morning I feel like I have awakened from an induced sleep. I somehow lost sight of God. I looked at a pink rose I had picked. It was so perfect, someone asked if it was real. This morning I looked at it with a more thankful eye - the one God had given me. It is indeed so simply beautiful, it's fragrance pure and sweet. The lake water this morning was warm after so much rain and storm. Odie wanted a drink so I cupped my hands into his shallow bowl.

God is good - again. He never changes, he is forever the same - faithful, gracious, hopeful, eternally waiting. I was the one who had let my focus waver. How that changes us! How much richer is my world when I allow God to show it to me through his eyes and heart. Ask him for his gift of vision, let all things be new again.

July 14th
Young Mink

This morning, while waiting for the sun to burn through the clouds, I watched a young mink wander through the rocks. He is familiar with every hidden crevice and path behind the boulders. He would appear in the ivy and disappear again. Like any puppy, he chased his tail, yawned, and circled and stretched out, sleepy on the warm rock surface. And yet, he is feared by all the water fowl and hated by property owners for his destructive behavior. He is vicious when cornered and attacks the vulnerable young.

The big question is – How and why does God allow evil in this world?

July 15th

Momma Calling

I awoke to hearing Momma calling me - quack, quack... quack, quack. Today was supposed to be overcast and rainy, but the sun was glinting off the water. I have made an effort to show the ducks the seed falling from my hand. They are aware of me throwing it. In the early days their tolerance of my presence was because of the seed floating on the water. Now they all watch my hand and will come close to feeding from it. Only once this year has Momma eaten from my hand. I got to enjoy Momma with her three young ones and one of her's from last year with her four. The youngest lost one has been adopted and is tolerated in this group. I am hoping this is the family that will come to my hand. Momma feels safe enough to fly up on the jetty and peck at scattered seed. Sometimes I marvel and wonder that they trust me enough to be so vulnerable.

How God must be satisfied when he sees us, sees our willingness to trust him, to be open enough for him to share with us.

July 16th

Poppa and Dinty

Poppa and Dinty have come to exemplify much in our world. Their "bully-ness" spoils the community that so often gathers together. Each family maintains a closeness to each other and a distance from others. They all, for the most part, tolerate each other. When Poppa and Dinty arrive, all the young literally run and scurry along the surface to get away as quickly as they can. Momma will hold her place for awhile before she wanders off. Young momma with the most young leaves immediately. She made the determination in the very beginning never to be around them. She had eight babies in the beginning, now only four and the orphan. Life has been dangerous - and cruel.

If I try to scare Poppa and Dinty away, it affects them all, so I try to feed them on the other side of the jetty and I throw seed in the opposite direction to distract them from becoming aggressive, again.

God loves all people, even the bullies, but I wonder if the rewards are for those who manage to live together, to doing life together. Those who abuse God's trust will one day be desperately alone.

July 17th

Untrusting

The dog needed out early this morning so I was at the dock at 6:30, not my usual time. New ducks were there but not so new that they didn't recognize that I was the one who fed them. Momma saw me from a distance and flew up on the grass behind me. She followed me to the jetty but hesitated because I was too close to it. So I backed away. She disappointed me and I was annoyed that she is still untrusting.

How does God feel when it appears we would all accept his gifts and his blessings but refuse to enter into a real relationship with him? Are we afraid he'll grab hold of us and never let us go? How sad he must feel to see us shrink away from his overtures to us. Fellowship with God and following his wise council should be our purpose in life. Through Him all things are possible. Who would turn down such a wonderful gift?

July 18th
Breakthrough!

Breakthrough this afternoon! The largest two of Momma's young ate out of my hand. (It's the middle of July.) My back was aching from being bent over for so long but it was worth it. They had been skimming loose seed off the bottom and getting so close they would bump against me. I tentatively touched a flipper, then a chest, then the largest one darted seed out of my hand. The smallest one, and surprisingly, momma, held back. I heard the distress peep from the orphan coming closer. Momma nipped at it and chased it away. Only yesterday it was included and tolerated in the group. How could Momma turn on it like that?

I am feeling impatient with her. She gives a quiet hiss in her throat to warn me or let me know she isn't comfortable, yet she'll fly up not a foot from me and sit down to peck at seed. She reminds me of Rebecca - she arranges everything for her favorites.

How does God remain so fair, so faithfully just? He loves all and blesses many. Do you recognize him?

July 19th
Risky Storm

The weather today has been very changeable. The winds have shifted direction all morning. A storm advisory has been issued. The sun has tried to burn through the clouds without success. The sky has become darker, with strange overlaying cloud formations, the wind strengthening. Thunder is rumbling all around us. We have been watching a new family out in their boat, with four children delighting in jumping the waves in a tube. They have been heedless of the changing weather – the threat of extreme conditions. We shouted at them and waved them in. The father finally conceded to the dark downpour and came in to his dock.

Is he thankful for our warning/interference? Or was he enjoying his reckless challenge? Are you willing to risk everything to follow your own ways?

July 20th

God's Display

This was one of those still, perfect, quiet holiday mornings when I didn't mind getting up before anyone else. The water was like glass, birds quietly chattering. It was so still you could hear the ducks' feathers as they stretched their wings. I watched a beautiful young female preening herself – stretching and fanning her wings, elongating her neck to smooth her back. She was a moving piece of art, the display of patterns and feathers and teal iridescence was compelling to watch. No wonder native peoples adorned themselves with feathers.

What wisdom am I to glean from this display? I think it is God's completeness, that there is no detail so small he has not thought of it. This was one of those times you would like to be able to resurrect when life is on the brink of chaos, so you could feel that complete certainty and peace instead of all the uneven entanglement life is most of the time.

Is your faith in God enough to sustain you when

his perfection is remote, too far away for you to grasp, when everything you see is shouting he's abandoned you? God's Word says no one will be tested beyond what they are capable of carrying. So much that is seen in the world today – and in our own families and relationships – would seem to refute that.

So hold onto those moments of God's grace, those moments he gives you of his certain plan, his certain knowledge of you, his certain love of your life.

July 21st

Life Our Way

When we try to do life our own way and all we do is antagonize others and show our worst side, could be the very time God is trying to show himself to us. He offers a better way – a way of heart-healing and a new way of doing life. He is always ready to steady us and pick us up. He gave us a spirit that cannot be destroyed. He planted the seeds of hope and determination deep in our souls. Call on that inner gift of strength and recognize God the Giver.

July 22nd

Swimming with Oars

While relaxing and gazing at the afternoon horizon, I became aware of the game in the lagoon – when two ducks "swim with oars" in circles to test each other – only this game was longer and the bodies were submerged too long – round and round – splashing and squawking. Then Momma popped to the surface and the young mink swam into the rocks. His inexperience and Momma's maturity probably saved her. I could tell by the teal feather trail he had had her by the wing and tried to drag her under. Her sheer determination and strength saved her.

July 23rd

Test the Water

Another day with the water like glass, with just the gentlest of breezes rippling the surface. It was quiet enough that I could hear a young mother with a toddler at the beach. She was holding him and swinging his feet in the water, back and forth. Her words encouraged him, his response was delighted laughter. So another child will grow to love the lake.

Over the last while we have heard many responses. Some parents carry frightened children into deep water trying to make them be strong and unafraid, only to sear mistrust into their small bodies. Some hold and bob with children, singing and playing while the child gets used to the water.

Were you taken kicking and screaming in over your head?

No matter what your life experience has been, Jesus calls all of us with the same heart.

Come to me, all you who are weary and carry heavy burdens and I will give you rest. Take my yoke upon you. Let me teach you for I am humble and gentle and you will find rest for your souls. For my yoke fits perfectly, and the burden I give you is light.

Matthew 11:28–30

July 24th
Chipmunk

He will not crush those who are weak,
or quench the smallest hope,
Until he brings full justice with his final victory.
And his name will be the hope of all the world.
Matthew 12:20-21

We have taken to leaving seed on the dock, for Momma who usually flies up in the evening or first thing in the morning. We have noticed a new ritual - after Momma is done, the morning doves will land and take some of what's left. After them we see the small red squirrel and the chipmunk. Even as we sit there, they will all come, right down to the tiniest wren I have ever seen, not much larger than a humming bird. It takes the tiny seeds that all the others have overlooked or rejected as too small.

The Lord will not quench even the smallest hope. It is his gentle way that lets us see these smallest of patterns.

July 26th

Brazen Mink

One afternoon on the jetty, ducks were pecking at seed, two were on the dock, one was coming up the stairs. I was enjoying the quiet trust they had – kind of like the "Peaceable kingdom" when all of a sudden there was great flapping and quacking and all took flight. Somehow the mink got up under the step to the dock and darted out. I saw him so briefly and then he disappeared. What a brazen animal.

Later that afternoon, the group were all floating about fifteen feet from shore, bobbing with the current. Again, the outcry was made and all flew up in the air. I watched the mink, a strong swimmer, swim straight out from the rocks into deep water, thinking he could get them. Three near misses in as many days. Has he figured out how many come to be fed in the afternoon? I will have to be careful and watchful for the ducks.

There are times when I feel I have been drawn into uncomfortable territory by God, when things are unfamiliar and other's responses are unknown. God's Word gives us the same defenses that calls the ducks into flight. Exercise the power behind the knowledge of his word.

Trust in the Lord with all your heart, and do not lean on your own understanding. In all your ways acknowledge him, and he will make straight your path.
Proverbs 3:5-6

July 28th

Interaction

I have been thinking about Momma, and how our interaction started this collection. I have been thinking about her returning year after year and all her offspring returning too. Such is the connectedness of families. Her returning each year, unchanged and seemingly recognizing and trusting me, answers a deep hope we all keep in our hearts – that we are known and accepted in spite of all that happens to us and by us. I have watched her turn on her own now-grown offspring and attack their young with a fierceness that I find unsettling. She will nip a young one and take it to the bottom – long enough that I am afraid for it. This is my beloved Momma, the one I wait for each year. Even though I have seen her nasty side, I have not lost my delight in her.

So our Heavenly Father watches us and our acts of aggression , and unkindness, and willful disobedience. He does not lose his delight in us. He sees beyond our hurtful behaviors to a hope yet to be fulfilled.

God is light. In him there is no darkness.
1 John 1:5

July 29th

Feathers

I have been collecting feathers from the beginning; they are like found art to me. I have marveled at their shape, their silky texture, their subtle patterns. They are like the mystery of life itself - that all have a place and a purpose, a fit in the pattern of the cosmos. They represent the connectedness of us all in the earth - one leans and depends on another. The careful layering of patterns creates the beauty of the whole, whether it is a lady bug or a gliding eagle.

July 30th
Hot Summer

This a hot, dry week. The soft freshness of the morning air has evaporated by 9 a.m. The trees are so still, their leaves look almost tired. There is only the faintest movement on the water. This is the kind of day I remember as a child – too hot to go outside, we were soon bored. I remember looking through drapes drawn to keep the heat out, up to the cloudless blue sky, hoping to see a plane fly by so I would have something to watch.

We are not always challenged or in the excitement of spiritual awareness. Many days are like the still hot summer, when we can be lulled into inactivity, our senses dulled by the monotony of sameness in our days. We think "Wouldn't a thunderstorm be exciting?"

Even as I throw seed for the ducks today, they are only eating what is on the surface. None are diving for the seed lying on the sand. Are we so often like them, only willing to do life on the surface? Ask the Lord to take you to a deeper understanding, ask him to reveal more of himself to you. His passion will reawaken you and fill your days with meaning.

August 1st

Outstretched

In the cool of early morning, I decided to weed the front garden. As I sat in the shade taking a break, I was wondering what I would write about if the ducks hadn't come into my life. The shades of green, and overlapping shapes of leaves, the fragrance of the earth, the cedars and the sweetness of summer phlox I suppose. Lost in thought I watched a tiny insect fly up from a blade of grass. The grass bent under that tiny lift-off. There is that completeness of God again. In one of those "aha" moments I realized what it was about the ducks that drew me. It is their responsiveness, their willingness to interact, their individual personalities, their trust. That is also what draws us to God. He is looking for our response, our willing heart, our trust in him.

Later, at lunchtime, two young ones came on the dock for seed. Like any child, one tried to chase the other away. So the other waddled under the table where he couldn't be reached. He stayed under our feet all through lunch, relaxed enough to lay down, preen his beautiful outstretched wings and doze in the shade. How honored I felt by his trust in being safe with us. So, honor your heavenly Father. Trust Him as your place of safety. He will nurture your heart, expand your thinking and engage you in His plans for your life.

August 3rd

Your Own Soul

Now I say to you that you are Peter, and upon this rock I will build my church, and all the powers of hell will not conquer it. And I will give you the keys of the Kingdom of Heaven. Whatever you lock on earth will be locked in heaven, and whatever you open on earth will be opened in heaven.
Matthew 16:18-19

If you try to keep your life for yourself, you will lose it. But if you give up your life for me, you will find true life. And how will you benefit if you gain the whole world and lose your own soul in the process? Is anything worth more than your soul?
Matthew 16:25-26

God gives us an incredible opportunity. Make the journey worth it.

August 4th

Summer Momma

Summer momma was at the dock early this morning with her two young ones. I know that she knows me but she wouldn't come close for seed. Later in the morning she flew up to the jetty looking for a hand-out. She sat and ate while the two young ones were peeping and looking for her. She is definitely one of last year's off-spring. Maybe she'll come closer when she sees the four males come in. it always takes one to make the first step, to be forward enough to be the leader and then the rest follow.

Whom do you look to for leadership? How confident are you in that choice?

Tune your ears to wisdom, and concentrate on understanding. Cry out for insight and understanding. Search for them as you would for lost money or hidden treasure. Then you will understand what it means to fear the Lord, and you will gain knowledge of God.

Proverbs 2:25

August 5th

Open Mind

When you are told something or given information without understanding it, it doesn't matter how many times you hear it, if understanding is not there. It doesn't matter if it is how to focus a camera, how to run a boat, or how to let God heal you. Each time you hear it is like the first time – it is foreign and obscure even if it is detailed, logical and right. It takes a decision of your will to make the effort to understand, to be willing to engage your mind and learn to follow – whether it's technical instructions or the heart and will of God. Opening your mind and heart is always the beginning of knowledge and new abilities.

So I advise you to live according to your new life in the Holy Spirit. Then you won't be doing what your sinful nature craves....But when the Holy Spirit controls our lives, he will produce this kind of fruit in us: love, joy, peace, patience, kindness, goodness, faithfulness, gentleness and self-control. Here there is no conflict with the law.
Galatians 5:16,22-23

August 8th
God's Perfect Order

As God delivered the people from slavery in Egypt, he offers us a way out of bondage in our own lives. Exodus 6:7 says – I will make you my own special people, and I will be your God.

He offers us his way to overcome the distresses and burdens in our lives. By focusing on God's creation and perfect order in the natural world, we can be reassured of his complete understanding and great care. He was so in control over the world that when he turned the Nile waters into blood – Exodus 7:19 says – Then the Lord said to Moses: "Tell Aaron to point his staff towards the waters of Egypt – all its rivers, canals, marshes, and reservoirs. Everywhere in Egypt the water will turn into blood, even the water stored in wooden bowls and stone pots in the people's homes."

The God that can so completely affect a nation can certainly affect the smallest of our own concerns. The rain he brings into our lives is meant to help us grow. He is able to work through even the storms that we have created ourselves. Ask him to be in your day, to guide your thoughts. You may find your feet walking in a new direction, you will find your heart changing. He will show you a hopeful world, he will lift your distress. He will free you from your heavy heart.

August 9th
Looking for God

This morning felt like such an ordinary day. I guess they can't all be stellar days. We have had high winds and crashing waves for a few days so the lake feels like fall when all the boaters and swimmers have gone. The waves brought in more sand to cover the exposed small rocks and zebra mussel shells that are so hard on bare feet. Wandering in the water, everything seemed bare, clean, and clear. There were no wonderful feathers to find. All was quiet. It felt like something had been abandoned.

Summer momma and her two young arrived. They looked at me with mistrust. I heard in my head - "And they did not know me." Does the Lord know our aloneness and our sadness? Has he felt firsthand our disappointment and grief?

Resolve to keep seeking him. Look for ways to make his heart joyful in you.

August 10th

Recognition

I seem to somehow have lost track of the ones who eat from my hand. There are now three gentle ones, almost mature, who look at me with such expectation, and take the seed I offer with real gentleness. Momma's four young can now fly up to the dock, although you can almost see them measuring the distance. They will feed next to me and sit down beside my feet. There are many new large males, their heads in transition from immature browns to brilliant greens. They are quick to realize this is a good place.

Our daily interaction created a trust, recognition gave reassurance, and knowing the reward created desire. The Lord desires your interaction. He waits for your trust, your recognition of his soverignty, your knowing of his character.

His delight in you is immeasurable, his patience will outlast you. Enter into a relationship that will be profound beyond your imagining.

August 11th

Perfection

It was overcast but warm today - perfect for picking berries. The heady fragrance of picking ripe blackberries mixed with wild mint as I pulled it out. Many branches that were heavy with fruit were well past picking, the berries shriveled in the heat. The branches that were hidden in the mint and bee balm shade were late ripening. I know I picked some questionable berries to make sure I had enough. As I rinsed and discarded stems and leaves, the occasional snail and ladybug, I started thinking - How many of these berries are truly perfect?

Sacrifices to God were to be perfect-, sheep, rams or doves without blemish. What journey or lengthy inspection would have had to happen to find a perfect sacrifice? As I sifted handfuls of berries, I discarded many past their prime, thinking about God's desire for perfection. It called for willingness and commitment; discipline and obedience. It called us to honour God and asked for humility in the offering. How many of us today would understand the command and be committed to the search and sacrificial giving back to God?

PERFECT(ED)(ION) (brought to) wholeness and completeness; describes whatever level of maturity or morality can be expected given human nature.

"I have given them the glory you gave me, so that they may be one, as we are – I in them and you in me, all being perfected into one. Then the world will know that you sent me and will understand that you love them as much as you love me.
John17:22

August 12th

Good Things

Keep me safe, O God,
For I have come to you for refuge.
I said to the Lord, "You are my master!
All the good things I have are from you."
Psalm 16:1-2

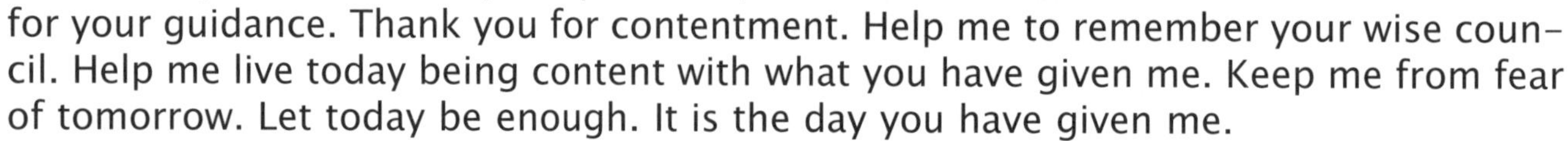

Yesterday was full of peace. Contentment and good decisions were mine. That is what God's blessing feels like to me.

Thank you, Lord, for your presence, for your guidance. Thank you for contentment. Help me to remember your wise council. Help me live today being content with what you have given me. Keep me from fear of tomorrow. Let today be enough. It is the day you have given me.

The land you have given me is a pleasant land.
What a wonderful inheritance!
I will bless the Lord who guides me;
Even at night my heart instructs me.
I know the Lord is always with me.
I will not be shaken, for he is right beside me.
Psalm 16:6-8

August 16th

Thirsty

These are the lazy days of summer. Only the truly diligent have green lawns and lush planters. Most lawns are now parched and planters are struggling. I have found it a contradiction having burned, dry grass on the edge of a large body of water - it is so enticingly near. Many people have pump systems to bring lake water for their gardens and lawns. It still requires effort to water daily to keep property lush and healthy. So many have the greatest of intentions and yet slip in their daily commitment.

God has such a vast spiritual reservoir for us but we must come to it - daily. He will feed your mind and water your soul.

Let the thirsty ones come - anyone who wants to.
Let them come and drink the water of life without charge.
Revelation22:17

If you are thirsty - come to me! If you believe in me, come and drink! For the Scriptures declare that rivers of living water flow out from within.
John 7:37

For I will give you abundant water to quench your thirst and to moisten your parched fields. And I will pour out my Spirit and my blessings on your children. They will thrive like watered grass, like willows on a riverbank.

Isaiah 44:3

August 18th
Letting Go

The subtle patterns of duck's feathers intrigue me. Each one, even on its own is interesting. How they are layered and shaped creates such beauty. Many see only a brownish bird but it has been the intricacy and simplicity of their feathers that spoke to me of God. That we are, each of us, so like these God-created feathers; each so different and yet all with the same needs, feelings, longings aches, and joys - just in a different arrangement.

When ducks are displaying and jostling for dominance, they grab at each other, sometimes pointedly at wings or behind the neck. Feathers often fly - floating over the water like small curved boats. I have amassed quite a collection; I see art in each one I have picked up. Yesterday there was quite a commotion as other

ducks have started to move along the lake - one of the first indicators of fall approaching. Three beautiful long side feathers floated out of my reach. Even my paddle was not long enough to reach them. The wind carried them out and away. I have had to learn to "let go" of them, knowing there'll be others.

We must all learn to let go. We must trust in the Lord's ability to provide for our today's and tomorrows. We must trust that he will bring to us what we need so we don't need to grab at every passing thing. Let him speak to you, show you what is important for you and what you need to let go of. His understanding of you is infinite, his desire to guide your life the most honorable and loving. Let go of your own frantic grip on life and let the Lord Almighty lead you. He gave his life for you.

August 22nd

Storm Sheer

The lake has been wild for days. Crashing, relentless waves made even sleep difficult. The roar of the wind and water was loud even with all the windows closed. Torn leaves and debris litter the lawn.

Sometimes the onslaught of life is just as relentless, overwhelming us and sapping our strength. How amazing that even in the midst of pounding waves, we can know the certainty of God's plans.

The Lord's strength will outlast anything this world can throw at you.

August 23rd
Cormorants

I just happened to look out this morning – at the very time a long line of cormorants was flying low over the water. Hundreds had collected and started their move along the lake. I watched for long minutes as groups kept passing – all following the others, so low to the water, so level with its undulating surface. It filled me with wonder that such sure timing and flight has happened for centuries. The count was probably in the thousands. How many other people over time just happened to stand up, to glance out over the water and witness this procession?

For centuries we have been called to witness for the Lord. We just happen to be somewhere, we just happen to stand up or glance over and the Lord gives us the vision of his grace as we see someone who needs his touch. Be amazed at his certain timing. Follow his glance. Tell others what they are longing to hear.

God arms me with strength;
he has made my way safe.
He makes me as sure-footed as a deer,
Leading me safely along the mountain heights.
He prepares me for battle;
He strengthens me to draw a bow of bronze.
Psalm 18:32

Through all of life's challenges, he stands with us, gives us strength and direction.

August 28th

Thank You Lord

Thank you Lord, for the still quietness of each early morning. For the peace and freshness floating over the lake. For the clarity and uncomplicated joy of its newness. As the complications of this world invade my day, Lord help me keep a place in my mind pure and clear, that place where you teach me and remind me of your ways.

The law of the Lord is perfect, Reviving the soul.
The decrees of the Lord are trustworthy, Making wise the simple.
The commandments of the Lord are right, Bringing joy to the heart.
The commands of the Lord are clear, Giving insight to life.
Reverence for the Lord is pure, Lasting forever.
The laws of the Lord are true, Each one is fair.
Psalm 19:7-9

There is salvation in no one else! There is no other name in all of heaven for people to call on to save them.
Acts 4:12

August 30th

Geese

Canada geese flew out over the bay this morning. A man and his dog have been given the job of clearing them off the beach. The geese all take flight together, usually circling over the treetops of the park. I have seen them resting in farmer's fields and on ponds near grazing cattle. When they decide to return to the beach, it is yet the same group descending and coasting into the shore. I often wonder what it is like to be so completely part of a group.

September 3rd
Fire on the Altar

Remember, the fire must be kept burning on the altar at all times.
It must never go out.
Leviticus 6:13

My ducks seem to have gone somewhere. They have been gone over a week. The lake seems silent – the quiet the unsought beginnings of fall. Even the air is softer and the sun's intensity is lessening. There is one lone youngster, one of the last four babies who has been sleeping on the sand next door. He was probably separated from the rest by the high winds and waves last week. I have missed their chatter and their regular appearance each morning.

We were out in our paddleboat this afternoon, enjoying the sunshine and blue sky. As I let my foot drift along in the water, God somehow touched my thoughts and I was overwhelmed by his abundance – the warmth of the sun, the freshness of the water, its fragrance in the air – the place and moment such a gift.

Remember, the fire must be kept burning on the altar at all times. It must never go out.

September 4th

With Your Own Hand

Present it to him with your own hands as an offering given to the Lord by fire.
Leviticus 7:30

As I re-read these thoughts that have called to me over the last year. I have realized that God calls us to discover him. He knew I would understand his character as he revealed it through my feeding of the ducks. We must all find our own way to God - that he wants us to know him is amazing enough! But to realize he understands you so well that he will show you through something very personal and real to you is discovery in itself. You are the only person who can know God in the way he will speak to you. With your own mind and heart ask him to reveal himself to you. The time spent in reading God's Word, in reflection and watching for him will enrich your life and take you on a journey only God the Creator could orchestrate.

September 7th

None Should Perish

The air this morning was hot and humid and very breezy. It was so warm I wanted to pull it around me like the softest, warmest blanket. It was so comfortably warm against my face, it felt almost like a kitten's fur. It reminded me of an old Cat Stevens song - "May my arms surround you like the sea surrounds the shore." I just sat listening to the rolling waves and hot wind.

Later that afternoon I was sitting on the step with seed on the ground in front of me. The last two young ones flew up! Their wings were still so undeveloped I wondered how they could fly south with the rest. As they ate the seed, the hot wind kept blowing, almost rolling them over. Their feathers were ruffled in all directions. They had to lie down with the force of the wind. What felt balmy to me was a battle for them to remain upright. I would have loved to pick them up and smooth their feathers and shelter them but they, of course, would have been traumatized by my actions.

Sometimes we can't shield those we love by our own experience. Each of us must experience life as it is given to us. Recognize the ones who stand watch for you and be thankful for their attention.

You may think God is nowhere in sight. The winds may be stronger than you think you can handle. You may be battling to keep yourself upright. God's desire is that none should perish.

If a shepherd has one hundred sheep, and one wanders away and is lost, what will he do? Won't he leave the ninety-nine others and go out into the hills and search for the lost one? And if he finds it, he will surely rejoice over it more than over the ninety-nine that didn't wander away. In the same way, it is not my heavenly Father's will that even one of these little ones should perish.

Matthew 18:12-14

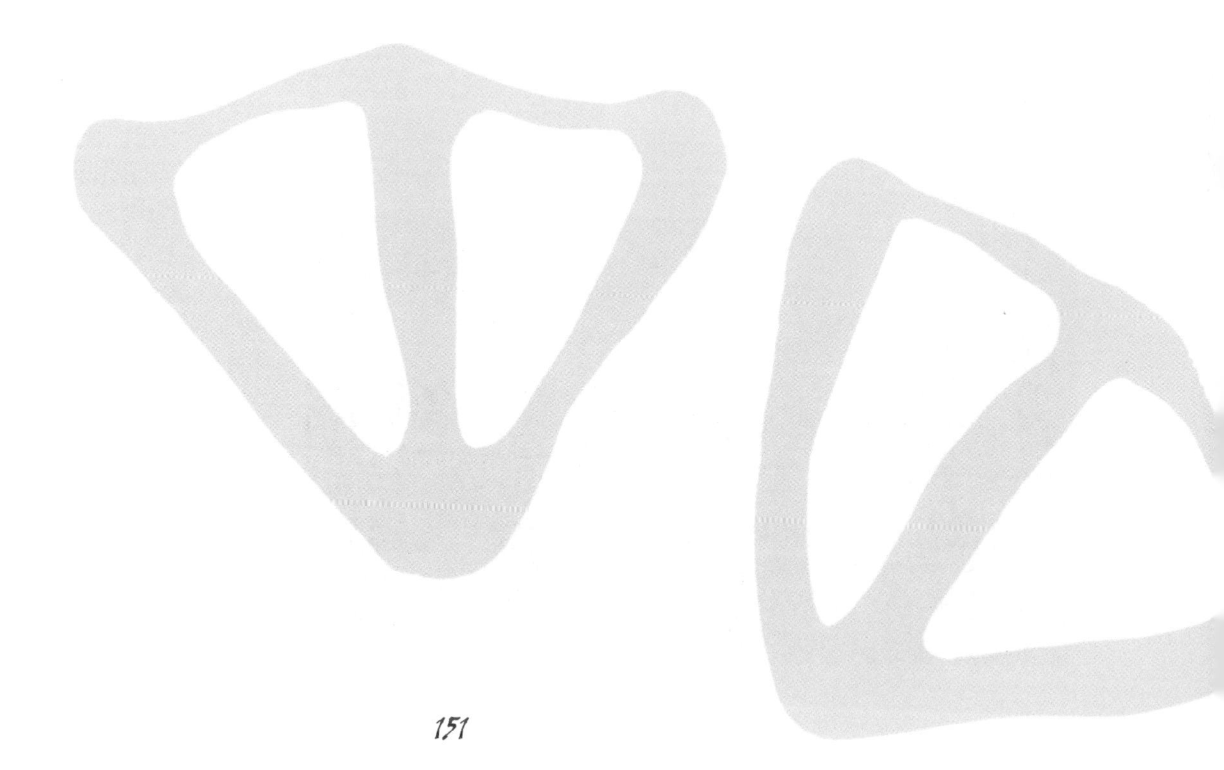

September 10th

Fall Rains

Fall rains have begun. All night we could hear raindrops beating on the roof and this morning they are dripping from the trees. The grass is greening in the cooler air. How desperately the rain was needed over the summer but here it is at the end of the season. There is a comfort in the eternal progression of the seasons. Even watching the collection of birds along the lake holds a reassurance in what has been for thousands of years. This rhythm in life gives us a framework – of expectations, of goals, of measuring our own progress.

Fall is a time of thanksgiving. When the sun returns and days are warm and fragrant with falling leaves, we can sit and reflect on the fruits of our labour – whether it's in having cultivated a garden, or having watched children grow in the sun. The change of seasons witnesses God's certain assurance that as day follows night, his presence is eternally certain and secure.

September 17th

Thanksgiving

The lake's horizon is hidden this morning in vapor swirling off the surface. The air is crisp and clear. As much as it is beautiful, I look at it with reluctance – gone will be the warm stone sidewalk under bare feet, the call of waiting ducks at the jetty, the hot afternoon breezes. We still will have some warm days but they will be the exception. They will come like stolen moments from winter's approach.

Summer is so uncomplicated, it's freedom and joy so easily perceived. Autumn is a time of planning and preparation for winter. How I dread the cold and silence of the ice.

Do not let darkness rob you of the goodness of God's light. Cherish the memories, remember the strength of the sun, keep your heart warm, prepared for his council. Nothing can separate you from the love of God. Remember that God walks with you throughout your life. His warmth and his strength with sustain you through the winters. The God of all the earth will never let the fire go out.

September 19th

The Stone Path

I thought my time of feeding the ducks was over. Only bossy and her two young bossies were around. They came close to the jetty wall yesterday but most of the seed I threw was swallowed by the waves. So much of God's gifts to us get swallowed up by our concerns in life. We often won't make the effort because of obstacles and objections.

This morning the waves have somewhat calmed so I was trying to decide whether to go and look for any ducks. To my surprise the bossies were on the lawn under the feeder, picking through the grass. As I gently opened the door they scattered. As the seed bounced over the sidewalk they ventured up for breakfast. It made the blue jays squawk to see them eat their portion of seed.

Do you see other's being blessed and wonder why you aren't experiencing the same things? God's desire is that none should perish. He may have placed something on the path ahead of you. Claim what he is offering, learn to be grateful for small things.

September 20th

God's Family

I realized today how happy it makes me to see a momma and her family arrive and feed together. It restores something in me that has been bruised. I have seen the respect of a new courting pair, the attention and devotion to each other touches me. It has given me peace to see a family grow that has stayed together over the summer. I have been delighted by the return of grown offspring and their young - that they return to the same spot, that they recognize and are familiar with a safe place.

This is God's heart for each of us - to love and care for each other, through all the seasons of life; that we should return to each other - that place of familiarity and safety - that place where our souls are recognized, where bruises get to be healed. Our own families are meant to be part of that larger family of God.

"By his wounds we are healed."

Jesus will redeem your bruised and broken heart. I believe his spirit is so grieved by all of our bruises, whether they are physical or spiritual. Seek Him in all you do, be open to the Healer of your soul.

To you, O Lord, I lift up my soul.
I trust in you, my God!
Do not let me be disgraced,
Or let my enemies rejoice in my defeat.
No one who trusts in you will ever be disgraced,
But disgrace comes to those who try to deceive others.
Show me the path where I should walk, O Lord;
Point out the right road for me to follow.
Lead me by your truth and teach me,
For you are the God who saves me.
All day long I put my hope in you.
Psalm 25:1-5

There are those who love you, those who have been given the eyes and heart of God for you.

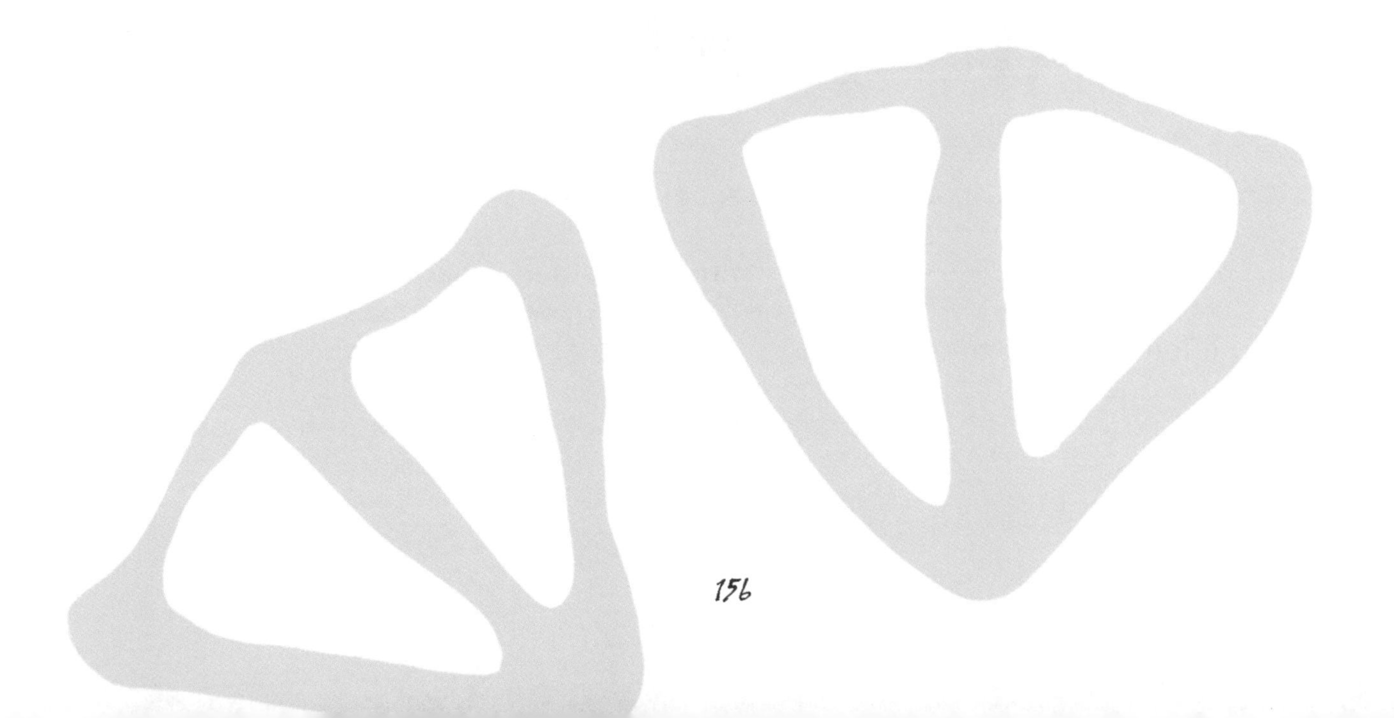

My prayer for you is that as you meet with others, that the Lord's presence would be in your hearts, that there would be love and understanding and God's wisdom in your midst; that you would experience his comfort and his healing spirit in your hearts and minds; his healing presence in your bodies, over all your hurts. I pray he will make you aware of all his gifts that surround you.

I wish you sun-filled days and peaceful waters.

I wish you God's amazing eternity.

Jesus prays for future believers
I am praying not only for these disciples but also for all
who will ever believe in me because of their testimony.
My prayer for all of them is that they will be one, just as you and I are one,
Father - that just as you are in me and I am in you, so they will be in us,
and the world will believe you sent me.
John 17:21